**ROBERT SWINDELLS**

CORNELSEN
SENIOR
**ENGLISH**
LIBRARY

# Daz 4 Zoe

**Cornelsen**

Robert Swindells **Daz 4 Zoe**

**Herausgegeben von:**
Birgit Ohmsieder

**Verlagsredaktion:**
Katrin Heinecke

**Technische Umsetzung:**
Britta Dieterle, Buch und Gestaltung

**Umschlaggestaltung:**
Cornelsen Verlag Design; *Bildrecherche*: Josephine Wolff

**Umschlagfoto:**
© Dex Image / Getty Images

**www.cornelsen.de**

1. Auflage, 1. Druck 2012

Alle Drucke dieser Auflage sind inhaltlich unverändert
und können im Unterricht nebeneinander verwendet werden.

**© 2012 Cornelsen Verlag, Berlin**

Druck: Drogowiec-PL Spolka z o. o., Kielce

ISBN 978-3-06-033143-7

 Inhalt gedruckt auf säurefreiem Papier aus nachhaltiger Forstwirtschaft.

# CONTENTS

## Abbreviations and Annotations

| | | | | |
|---|---|---|---|---|
| **adj** | adjective | | **fml** | formal |
| **adv** | adverb | | **infml** | informal |
| **AE** | American English | | **jdm./jdn.** | jemandem/en |
| **BE** | British English | | **n** | noun |
| **ca.** | circa; about | | **sb.** | somebody |
| **cf.** | confer; see | | **sl** | slang |
| **e.g.** | exempli gratia; for example | | **sth.** | something |
| **esp.** | especially | | **usu.** | usually |
| **etc.** | et cetera; and so on | | **v** | verb |

The annotations are arranged chronologically; the first time a word is used is where you will find it explained.

# A TRUE STORY

Palm trees don't like the cold. That's why they don't occur naturally in England. You see them sometimes in seaside towns but they never look right. Ragged they are, with dead bits hanging down.

5   Old people occur naturally in England, but they don't like the cold, either. Some of them are ragged too, and there are probably dead bits only you don't see them.

Anyway, there was this winter. It was a really cold winter – one of the coldest on record – with hard frosts every night. It was so cold that old people started dying. Daren't have the fire on, see. Not with
10   electricity the price it was. So they wrapped themselves up in blankets and sat shivering till they fell asleep and died, like lost explorers in the Arctic.

And there was this seaside town that had some palm trees. Now palm trees can't feel the cold, but it kills them just the same. It was
15   killing these particular palm trees all right. Slowly but surely.

Until one day the man that looked after them – the Town Gardener, I suppose – had this brilliant idea. What he did was, he got a lot of electric blankets and some very long cables and he plugged the blankets in and ran them out on the long cables and
20   wrapped them round the palm trees. It took several blankets to wrap each tree but when he switched on, the trees were really snug.

Every night the Town Gardener switched on, and night after night the electricity ran through the long cables, warming the blankets till the cold spell was over and the palm trees were saved.

25   Afterwards it was on telly and in the papers, how the palm trees were saved. What a good idea, people said. What a clever man. Everybody was really happy.

Well, no – not everybody. Some of the old folks – some of them that didn't die – moaned on about the waste of electricity, but you're

---

3 **ragged** (adj) ['rægɪd]: torn, having an uneven outline   19 **plug sth. in**: connect a piece of electrical equipment to sth. (e. g. the main supply of electricity)   21 **snug**: warm and comfortable   24 **spell** (n): short period of time   29 **moan** (v, infml): complain

going to get moaners whatever you do, and the moral of the story is you can't please everybody.

Or is it?

The rest of this book is fiction but it could come true, and we wouldn't like it if it did. You'll see what I mean when you've read it.  5 It could come true, but it won't if we're together. All of us.

There's no reason why we shouldn't be.

# DAZ

Daz thay call me. 2 years back wen I com 13 Del that's my brovver   2
thay catch im raiding wiv the Dred. Top im don't thay, and im just
gon 15.

5    2 lornorders com tel our mam, 1 wumin, 1 man, nor thay don't
come til after thay dunnit neever. Our Mam been down a longtime
fore then wiv the dulleye, and she just sort of stairs dont she, til thay
go of, and its not til nite she crys.

She sez dont you never go of wiv no Dred, our Daz.

No Mam, I sez, but I never crost my hart. Don't cownt less you
10   crost yor hart, rite?

2 **raid** (v) [reɪd]: enter a place, usu. using force, and steal from it   **top sb.** (infml):
kill sb.   2–3 **just gone 15**: just past 15   4 **lornorders = law and orders**: police
**mam**: mother   6 **dulleye**: depression

# ZOE

Hi. I'm Zoe. Zoe May Askew. Or Zoe may not. (Joke!) I'm fourteen. My friend at school is Tabitha. Tabitha Flinders Wentworth for short. She's fourteen too. If the name seems familiar to you it's no big surprise. Her dad's Paul Wentworth of Wentworth and Lodge (Developments) PLC, the outfit that shoved up practically every 5 residential estate in practically every suburb in England. You're bound to have seen their boards, plus their ads on T.V. He's into about a million other things too, Tabby says. Security. Roads. Power. *Elektrik* He's into power all right. Chair of the Suburb Selectmen, Chair of Schools Management Committee, etcetera, etcetera, etcetera. Dog 10 leaves a mess on the sidewalk, Paul Wentworth'll make himself Chair of it.

They're loaded. Well, you can imagine. They live in this gorgeous architect-designed house on Wentworth Drive. That's right – Wentworth Drive. He built the place and named it after himself, and why 15 not?

I know what you're wondering. You're wondering how come Tabby Wentworth would bother with a scumbag like me, right? Sure you are. Well, my dad's an estate agent, see, and what estate agents do is they sell houses. You probably thought they sold cheeseburgers, 20 but they sell houses. Wentworth builds 'em, Dad sells 'em. They're not friends, exactly, but they do a lot of business together and that's what it's all about, isn't it?

Well, no, as a matter of fact, it's not.

Listen. I want to tell you a story, only I've got to start at the 25 beginning, right? And that's where Tabby Wentworth comes in. At the beginning. Because she started it. She started it because everything's boring and fourteen's a lousy age and chippying's about the

---

5 **shove sth. up** (infml): *etwas (irgendwo) hinklotzen (ugs.)*   6 **residential estate**: area consisting mainly of houses where people live   9 **chair**: *Vorsitzende(r)* **Selectman**: one of a board of officials elected to serve as the chief administrative authority   13 **loaded** (infml): rich   **gorgeous** ['gɔːdʒəs]: lovely   18 **scumbag** (sl): unpleasant person

only way you can get a bit of excitement around here. Chippying. If
you've never heard of it, don't worry. You will. In fact you're going to
know all about chippying real soon.

* * *

There's us and there's them, see? Subbies and Chippies. They don't
5 call themselves Chippies, of course. I don't know what they call
themselves, but I know they call us Subbies. That's because we live
in the suburbs. We work and take showers and have nice houses.
They don't. They hang out and live in crummy apartments and they
don't even wash, for Pete's sake. And they hate us. We're just
10 ordinary, decent people, doing pretty much what people ought to
do, but they hate us. Dad reckons it's envy. They envy us. They want
our cars and our money and our nice houses, but they don't want
our long years in school and they don't want to work. That's what
Dad says, anyway. I don't know. I bet they're the same as everybody
15 else, really, but I wouldn't say that to Dad. He says they get so many
handouts they don't need to work. And if they want some money or
a nice car, they just sneak into the nearest suburb and take it. That's
why we have fences and lights and guards. That's how come we have
to carry ID all the time, and why we keep moving if we go outside.
20     Say you have an aunt or a cousin or somebody living in a neigh-
bouring suburb and you want to visit with them. What you have to
do is get in the car, check the tank, hit the freeway with your foot
down and go like the clappers till you're there. It's the only way. You
stop out there – you just so much as slow down – and they got you.
25 They're watching all the time, see. All the time.
    Why Chippies, I hear you ask. Why do we call them Chippies.
Well, that's easy. It's their favourite food, chips. They practically live
on them. Everybody knows that. It's a well-known fact. And that's
where chippying comes from. It means going out and mixing with
30 the Chippies.

---

9 **for Pete's sake**: used when you are annoyed about sth.   16 **handout**: financial
support from the government   23 **like the clappers** (BE infml): very fast

What happens is, some kid gets fed up being cooped up. I mean all right – a suburb's a pretty nice place. I'm not saying that. But any place with a fence around'll get to you, eventually. So this kid gets ballsed off and he calls a couple of buddies and they get in the car and go. Not down the freeway, 'cause that only takes you to the next ⁵ nice prison. No. They take one of the turnoffs the copcars use and cruise into town. I mean right down there where the streets are dark and dirty with high, crummy buildings and broken glass everywhere. Why? Because the one thing those dumb Chippies know how to do is have a good time. ₁₀

They have these clubs. Not like our clubs. I'm not talking about squash clubs or health clubs or bridge clubs, and I'm not talking about youth clubs, either, with bands that play gospel half the time. No. These clubs're night-clubs. You know. Dim, smoky little joints with booze and dope and bands that really belt it out. All the stuff ₁₅ the Chippies knock off, stuff they lift in the suburbs or take from hi-jack trucks gets fenced in the clubs. You might have seen something similar in old movies, but unless you chippy you're never gonna see one for real.

And that's where the kids go. Round the clubs. And if you think ₂₀ that's safe you're crazy. It's not safe. In fact it's downright dangerous, but that's all part of the fun.

The reason it's dangerous is, two reasons. First, you've got money and they don't, and they know you have it, and there's a lot of them and only a few of you. And second, they hate you anyway, cause ₂₅ you're a Subby and they'd as soon kill a Subby as look at him.

So yes, it's dangerous, but you've got one thing going for you and it's this. You're here to spend money. Cash money, and cash is scarcer than hen's teeth in Chippyville. They call it peanuts. They'll kill for it, but killing brings the cops and they'd rather get it some other way. ₃₀ You spend it, they got it. You have a good time spending it, you're

---

1 **coop sb. up**: keep sb. inside a building or in a small space    4 **be ballsed off** (sl):
be completely fed up with sth.    8 **crummy** (infml): in a bad condition
15 **booze** (infml): alcohol    **dope** (infml): a drug    **belt sth. out**: sing a song or play
music loudly    16 **knock sth. off** (BE sl): steal sth.    **lift sth.** (infml): steal sth.
28 **scarce**: *knapp*

gonna come back again. And again. And again. And even a dumb Chippy knows you don't kill the goose that lays the golden eggs. So, as long as you tread soft and don't go looking for trouble, you should be okay.

5  I say should be, because every now and then a Subby'll disappear while chippying. Sometimes a whole carful goes out and never comes back. They've probably run into a Dred squad, or some guy looking for a fight. You can never be sure, see, and that's where the kick is. Right down there where the butterflies play.

10  Anyway, I'm going to tell you what happened the night Tabby and me went out. The night it all began, only Daz wants to say a bit first. It will be a bit 'cause he doesn't write too good but I wish you could see him. Your knees'd go weak, he's so brilliant.

---

3 **tread soft** (infml) [tred]: try not to be noticed   9 **kick** (infml): strong feeling of excitement   **where the butterflies play**: cf. saying 'have butterflies in your stomach' (be nervous)

# DAZ

**4**  Don't you never go of wiv no Dred our mam sez, but wot woud you
do eh? How woud you feal if you was 1 of us.

We do wot we can rite. We do. You cant graft if ther is non and
ther is non. And its not easy to get a barf neever. Not wivout water
its not, and we dont hav water a lot of the time.                              5

And thay sit up ther in veezavill, larfin and telling each ovver
how them Chippys never graft and them Chippys never wash and
them Chippys do this and them Chippys do that and them Chippys
do the ovver. Its alrite for them innit. They got graft. Water. Peanuts.
Its alrite for them wiv all them fast motors and brand new doodys.          10
They mite wel larf wiv ther hi fences and dazzlers and bouncers
garding them and al that. i'd larf.

It'd be bad enuf if thay staid behind ther fences but thay dont.
Not all ov them. Sum com owt at nite, Chippying. Thats wot thay
call it – Chippying. Means coming down ahrend, clubbing. Thay got        15
clubs. Posh clubs, but thay got to come snooping in ars dont thay,
giving it the la-di-la and larfin. Thay got peanuts to buy the best
booze and get of wiv ar wimmin. Were dirty and funny, rite. But not
ar wimmin. Thats diffrent innit.

I hate Subbys. Hate them. Mister James up at the school sez a          20
long time ago ther was no Subbys and fings wasnt so bad. Then
Brittan rite – Brittan won the fork lands and got grate and sum
people got to be Subbys and sum dint and that was us. So wot i fink
is, get rid of the Subbys and fings'll be better. Stands to reason
dunnit.                                                                                     25

And that's wot the Dreds all about. Killing Subbys.

You cant join til 15 and now I am so watch out you basteds i'll
show you topping our Del.

---

3 **graft** (BE, v, infml): work   10 **motor** (BE): car   **doodies** (sl, pl): clothes
11 **dazzler**: *Flutlichtscheinwerfer*   **bouncer**: security guard   15 **ahrend** = our end
17 **ladida** (adj, infml): speaking or behaving in a way that is not natural or sincere;
affected   22 **fork lands** = Falkland Islands

# ZOE

It was a Friday, I remember that, because when Tabby mentioned going out I thought, well, at least I won't have to be up for school tomorrow.

I'm not saying that was my first thought. It wasn't. I'm not that cool. My first thought was What? Who? Me?

It was ten to nine and we were parking our bikes.

I'm fitting my front wheel in the slot and thinking about nothing in particular and she says, 'Fancy coming out tonight?'

'Huh – where?'

'Out. O-U-T. You know – down town.'

'Chippying?' My voice is a sort of croak. I know kids chippy but nobody ever asked me before. It's a bit of a shock.

'Sure, chippying,' she says. 'What d'you think I meant?'

I looked at her. 'I didn't know you went out.'

'I don't tell you everything I do,' she says. 'And anyway I only went once before.'

'When?'

'Three weeks ago. Four of us, in Ned Volsted's car. There was Ned, Tim Bixby, Sara Fanshaw and me. It was brilliant.'

'Why didn't you tell me?'

She shrugs, doesn't answer. Instead she says 'You in, or not?'

'Who else is going?'

'Ned, Larry Turner and me. And you, of course.'

'I haven't said I'll come yet. What about Tim and Sara?'

'What about them?'

'Why aren't they going again?'

'How do I know? Busy, I guess.' She grins. 'Or chicken.'

'Why – did something happen? Something bad?'

---

11 **croak** (n): a rough low sound like the sound made by a frog   21 **shrug**: raise your shoulders and then drop them to show that you do not know or care about sth.
27 **chicken** (adj, infml): afraid to do sth.

She shakes her head. We're walking away from the bikes. 'Nothing happened. I told you – we had a great night. You in or out? I can get somebody else.'

'I don't like Larry Turner. He's a creep.'

'So?' She shoots me a dirty look. 'You don't have to marry the guy. Just sit in the same car is all.'

It was then I had the thought about not having to get up for school. I don't want to kid you – I was nervous. In fact I was scared. Also, I didn't know how I'd get away. What I'd tell my parents. I mean you can't say 'Oh, by the way, Dad, I'm off down town tonight with some of the kids. We thought we'd get drunk, do a little coke, maybe dance with some of them husky Chippy guys. Look for me around three a.m.'

A part of me was terrified, and yet I wanted to go. I did. I felt I should anyway, because Tabby asked me and maybe she'd cool off if I refused. Stop being my friend. I don't make friends easily and I don't think I could stand that. So I told myself I didn't have to get up for school tomorrow, and then I said okay, I was in.

And that's how it began.

We used my cousin as an alibi. That's really why Tabby invited me. I knew that. Last time they used Sara Fanshaw's sister but Sara wasn't coming this time. Tabby's nice and all, but she's a user if you know what I mean. My cousin Alice lives over in Fairlawn which is the suburb next to ours. It's four miles. Alice and Jim have a big place with ponies on it and Tabby loves to ride. My mother has taken us over there a few times so there was no problem when I told my folks. When it was time I said 'See you' and walked out and Ned picked me up at the end of the street. Easy peasy.

Ned's eighteen. He's in the sixth form. He's off to university in the autumn and says he won't be back. He's lived in Silverdale all his life and he reckons eighteen years in Silverdale's enough for anybody.

---

4 **creep** (infml): person that you dislike very much   11 **do coke** (infml): take cocaine   12 **husky** (AE) (of a man): big, strong and sexually attractive   28 **easy peasy** (BE infml): very easy

I don't know. Whatever he does he's going to end up living in some suburb, and I hear they're all the same.

We picked up Larry next. He's sixteen, which makes him two years older than Tabby and me. He's a weedy little guy with snaggle
5 teeth and zits, but his dad's a Silverdale Selectman and he thinks that makes him a star.

Tabby was waiting on the corner. She got in the back with me. The city's south of Silverdale but we were supposed to be heading west for Fairlawn, so we cruised along Westgate and stopped at the
10 barrier. Ned rolled down the window and we sat looking innocent as the bouncer on duty stuck his head in. Bouncer's Chippy for security guard.

'ID?' We passed him our cards. He flicked through them and handed them back.

15 'Destination?'

'Fairlawn.' Ned has this very open smile. 'We're off to ride ponies with Ms Wentworth's friends.'

The smile cut no ice. 'I don't care if you're off to ride giraffes with Dracula's uncle, kid. Stay on the freeway and keep moving, right?'

20 'Right.'

'Got gas?'

'Yessir. Full tank.'

'Coming back tonight?'

'Ah-ha.'

25 'Time?'

Ned shrugged. 'Eleven. Eleven-thirty. Depends.'

'Use this gate so we can check you in.'

'Right.'

The guy nodded to his friend in the gatehouse, the pole went up
30 and we were out, whooping and slapping one another on the back as Ned went up through the gears. We headed west till we were clear of Silverdale, then found a cop route going south.

---

4 **weedy** (BE infml): having a thin weak body    **snaggle-tooth** (infml): a tooth which sticks out or is a strange shape    5 **zit** (infml): a spot on the skin, esp. on the face    30 **whoop** (v): shout loudly because you are happy or excited    32 **cop** (infml): police officer

# DAZ

6   its 2 days after i com 15 i tork 2 Mick my mate. Wot do i do abowt
joining Dred, i arst.

i fought you'd never arst, he sez. Mick's in already, see.

Well i'm arsting now, i sez.

See Cal, he sez. Cal'll put you strait.                                        5

Wears he hang owt, i arst. This is friday morning rite, and we're
off up the school. i reckon its my last time cos i'm jacking it in wen i
get in Dred. Our mam wont like it but that's how it gos. I can rite
and reckon and Mister James sez i'd hav no chance in the Veeza-
Teeza so wot's the point? The Veeza-Teeza's this exam, rite? Once a   10
year exam. If you pass you get a veeza to go to Subby school. You do
gud ther and Zap! you're a Subby. About 2 kids pass each year. If
that many.

Once Mister James fought i mite go in 4 it but it dint workout.
Aniway who wants to be a Subby when you can be a Dred?            15

Blue Moon, sez Mick. Tonite. Blue Moon's this club. Nite club.
Bands and strippers and pool and that. Yor spos to be 16 but no
1 bovvers. i bin in lotsa times.

Wot's he luck like, i arst. Mick larfs. i'll be wiv you, he sez. i'll
introdooce you. He sez this in a Subby-type voice. Introdooce. He's a   20
bit of a pillock old Mick, but hes alrite.

Aniway that's how com i'm in the Blue Moon that nite when these
Subby kids com in and screw me up. i mean 1 of them dos. i'll fill
you in later, rite?

5 **put sb. straight** (about/on sth.): make sure that sb. knows the correct facts when
they have had the wrong impression   7 **reckon** (infml): think   **jack sth. in** (BE
infml): decide to stop doing sth., esp. your job   9 **reckon**: calculate   21 **pillock**
(BE sl): stupid person   23 **screw sb. up** (sl): upset or confuse sb. so much that they
are not able to deal with problems in their life   23–24 **fill sb. in on sth.**: tell sb.
about sth. that has happened

# ZOE

I'd never seen a city before, except on telly. You see them sometimes
on the news. Glimpses shot from fans or moving vehicles when
there's been a big robbery or a riot. Fan's helicopter in Chippy talk.
Helicopter has four syllables and they can't handle it. That's what
5  Dad says, anyway.

You get these glimpses and you can see they're a mess. And that's
how Rawhampton looked as we approached it. Derelict houses,
some burned out. Cracks in the road with weeds poking through.
Piles of brick and glass and cement everywhere, all smashed up. It
10 was hard to imagine what it must've been like in the old days, with
cars and crowds and big stores and a million lights, like cities you
see in ancient movies. Gran says she remembers the city that way
but it's hard to imagine.

Anyway, there we were, cruising in through the outskirts and it
15 was like dusk and you couldn't see too well. None of the street lights
was working and Ned had to slow right down to keep from ramming
piles of trash or driving into a hole or something. There were holes
everywhere. Deep ones, full of slimy water. Ned switched on the
headlamps, but it was that weird time halfway between daylight and
20 dark when headlamps aren't much help.

There didn't seem to be any people about at first. Just dogs. You
hear about the dogs on telly, how they hunt in packs through the
streets, killing Chippy kids and eating them. You might have heard
this sick joke:

25 Why did the dog eat the Chippy?

'Cause he was its Pal.

Pal – geddit?

They weren't in packs, the ones we saw. They were loners,
dashing across in front of us with their tails between their legs. Some

---

2 **glimpse** (n): a short look at sb. or sth.    7 **derelict** ['derəlıkt]: (esp. of land or
buildings) not used or cared for and in bad condition    8 **weed**: wild plant growing
where it is not wanted

were pretty big, though, and they were all thin, and you could easily imagine them going for you if you didn't have the car.

As we drove further in we passed through a so-called residential development – multi-storey apartment blocks scattered across a wilderness of long grass and overgrown pathways. Most of the 5 blocks were doorless and glassless and there was rubbish everywhere. Cans and bottles, plastic bags, filthy mattresses, the skeletons of baby-buggies, you name it.

And people. People leaning in doorways, shuffling along broken paths, framed in unglazed windows. Ragged men with their hands 10 in their pockets and stubble on their cheeks. Slag-bag women with greasy hair and shapeless legs. Thin kids with bare feet and vacant expressions, watching our car go by. I shivered, wondering how people could bear to live like this.

As we left the residential area behind and approached the old 15 commercial centre, I began to wonder how the Chippies could possibly have anything to offer us which was worth the awful risk of being here. If you want to know the truth I was scared. I mean, I knew the city wasn't going to be Disneyland or anything. I knew that before I came. And everybody knows chippying's dangerous. 20 They run videos on telly about seven hundred times a night, warning you. One of them shows a car with all four doors open and a shoe lying in the road. Just a shoe. But it was worse than I'd expected and that was because of the eyes. Chippy eyes. What they should do is, they should show a video of Chippies looking at the camera like 25 they looked at us that night. That cold, dead look with something behind it like waiting.

I said to nobody in particular, 'These clubs. What're they like?'

Tabby tittered. 'Dark. They're dark.'

'And noisy,' said Larry, twisting his stringy neck to look around at 30 us. 'Fantastically noisy.'

---

4 **multi-storey**: with many floors    8 **you name it**: *alles Mögliche*    11 **stubble**: hairs that grow on a man's face when he has not shaved    **slag-bag** (sl): insult for a person, usu. a girl, who has many sexual partners    29 **titter** (v): laugh quietly    30 **stringy** ['strɪŋi]: thin so that you can see the muscles

'They're usually full of smoke, too,' Ned added. 'Your eyes start streaming after a bit.'

'So what's good about them?' I pursued. 'I mean, it seems a lot of hassle just to get deafened, choked and blinded. You could fall in a
5  cement mixer and have all the same stuff going for you.'

Ned laughed. 'I like it.' He looked at Tabby through his mirror. 'Your friend's a real wit, Tab.'

Tabby nodded. 'I know. That's why she's along.'

'Anyway.' The reflected eyes switched to me. 'You're about to find
10  out for yourself, Zoe. We're here.'

* * *

Ned steered the car into the curb and stopped. I looked out and saw what looked like a poky old shop in a dilapidated row. Its window was boarded up and somebody had daubed 'Blue Moon' across the boards with blue paint. The paint had run down in lines so that the
15  words seemed propped on spindly legs. Beside the window a door stood open and the strip of brickwork between supported a man in dark glasses who was chewing a match.

The man watched us get out of the car. As we approached the door he pushed himself upright and stood with his hands in his
20  pockets, blocking our way.

'Two bucks,' he mumbled. 'Each.'

Ned produced a handful of coins and began counting them into the man's palm. The guy rolled the match from one corner of his mouth to the other and said, 'Been saving up, kid?' Ned was
25  unloading small change on him and I guess he'd have preferred notes. With his shades and thin moustache he looked sort of sinister. I wouldn't have risked answering back, but Ned said, 'It's money isn't it?' and the guy just shrugged.

---

3 **pursue sth.**: continue to discuss sth.   4 **hassle** (n, infml): situation that is annoying   7 **wit**: clever and amusing person   11 **curb** (AE; BE: kerb): *Bordstein-kante*   12 **poky**: very small   **dilapidated** [dɪˈlæpɪdeɪtɪd]: old and in very bad condition   15 **prop** (v): support   **spindly** (infml): very long and thin; not strong
26 **sinister**: seeming evil or dangerous

All the time Ned was counting, people kept going in the door. Larry noticed this and said, 'Hey!' The man's eyes flicked up.

'Whassamarra, kid?'

'Them.' Larry pointed at two guys just walking in.

'What about them?'                                                                  5

'What about 'em?'

'They haven't paid. Why do we have to pay and not them?'

The guy sneered. 'What they gonna pay with, kid – food stamps? Subbies got all the peanuts.'

Chippies hardly ever get cash. Even I know that, for Pete's sake.   10
For all that he's the son of a Selectman, Larry can be very dumb sometimes.

When the guy finally let us in we followed Ned along a short passage into a large, crowded room. People sat hunched over little tables with drinks in front of them, and most of the space between   15
was filled with people standing. There was a bar along one wall and an alcove in another, stacked with sound equipment. A DJ was feeding an ancient twindeck. He had the volume so high you felt it through your feet. Near the alcove some people were trying to dance on a raised platform the size of a Kleenex. The atmosphere was   20
ninety percent smoke and there was a nauseating smell whose cause I didn't want to think about.

We were standing in the doorway. Ned turned and said something I didn't catch. I leaned toward him.

'What?'                                                                             25

He shoved his lips in my ear. 'I said, what'll you have?'

I didn't know. I wasn't concentrating. I'd seen a terrific-looking boy across the room. 'What's Tabby having?' I said.

'A lobotomiser.'

'A what?'                                                                           30

---

3 **whassamarra** = What's the matter?    8 **sneer** (at sb./sth.): show that you have
no respect for sb.    11 **for all that**: *obwohl*    14 **hunched**: *zusammengekauert*
17 **alcove** ['ælkəʊv]: *Nische*    18 **twindeck**: double cassette deck    21 **nauseate sb.**
['nɔːzieɪt]: make sb. feel that they want to vomit    27 **terrific** (infml): great
29 **lobotomise sb.**: make sb. less intelligent

'A lobotomiser. It's coke with rum and a couple of other ingredients. Try one?'

'Sure, why not?' I didn't want a drink. I specially didn't want a drink with a name like lobotomiser, but what could I do? I wanted to be part of the gang, and the quickest way to screw up something like that is to act like a drag.

So.

---

6 **drag** (n, infml): boring person

# DAZ

**8** Thay com in lucking nervous. 4 of em. 2 guys 2 wumen, nor thay aint old enuff 2 be owt ov school neever. Stop by the door lucking rownd like somfing smell bad. i'm wiv Mick and som ovver guys and we just turn away like we saying you noffing 2 us you Subby trash, only thers 1 of em rite, this girl, and she's nice. Not just 2 luck at.   5 i dont mean that. She coms in diffrent. Lucks rownd diffrent. Not sniffy if you know wot i mean. i cop a luck then turn away wiv the overs and then a bit later I luck rownd and catch er watching me. Soon as i turn er eyes go down but its 2 late i seen er. i gorra be careful cos i don't want Mick 2 see me lucking and him getting ready   10 2 introdoos me 2 Cal, but i keep watching owt ov my eye corner and she's fixt on me alrite.

---

7 **cop a look** (v): *heimlich einen Blick werfen*   12 **fix (your eyes, mind, etc.) on sb./sth.**: look at or think about sb./sth. a lot

# ZOE

Ned began making his way towards the bar and the rest of us
followed. The Chippies let us through, but they weren't acting
pleased to see us and I avoided looking in their eyes.

When we all had drinks, Ned used his height to look for space.
5 He spotted some and we went and stood there, holding our drinks
and surveying the scene.

It was no big deal, I can tell you that. Just a lot of mean, dirty
people crammed into a tacky room getting smashed, while some
psycho of a DJ took out their eardrums to get at their brains. I was
10 already wishing I hadn't come, and I knew if we got home in one
piece I was never going to do it again.

It must have shown on my face too, because Tabby nudged me
and grinned and pointed to my glass. 'Try it!' she yelled. 'It'll put you
in the mood.'

15 'Or in the hospital,' cried Larry, who looked drunk already.

I sniffed my glass, and it didn't smell like coke. I didn't want to
drink it, but I saw the evening in front of me and I sure didn't want
to spend all of it feeling the way I was feeling now. I shrugged, lifted
the glass to my lips and took a sip.

20 It wasn't bad. It tasted better than it smelled, and I could feel it
making its way down inside me like a hot little elevator. It felt sort of
good, if you want to know. I took another sip and that felt even
better. It was then I noticed the glass was dirty, but what a
lobotomiser'll do is, it'll relax you, right? Two sips and I was laid-
25 back to where I could think, what the heck d'you expect in a dive
like this – Waterford Crystal?

---

8 **tacky** (infml): cheap, in bad taste   **smashed** (sl): very drunk   9 **eardrum**:
*Trommelfell*   12 **nudge sb.**: push sb. gently in order to get their attention
24–25 **laid-back** (infml): relaxed   25 **what the heck** (infml): used to show that
you are surprised or annoyed   **dive** (n, infml): cheap, possibly dirty bar
26 **Waterford Crystal**: *edle Kristallglasmarke*

In fact it wasn't a bad old place once you got a drink inside you. It was sort of cheerful, really – all these people, laughing and smoking and moving to the music as if they weren't dirty or poor or anything. It was like they left all that outside. They were okay, and we were okay too. What you had to do was, you had to let go and let it sort of sweep you along. I was being swept along, all right. By the time I finished my drink all I knew was I never felt anything like this down the Silverdale youth centre. All of my nervousness had gone and I was ten feet tall. 5

I must have been on to my third lobotomiser when the boy I'd noticed before turned and looked at me. He was just another Chippy guy in a beat-up leather jacket and wild, greasy-looking hair, but he turned round and our eyes met and that was it. 10

I guess sometimes there are moments when people's lives change and they don't even know it. They can look back later, when everything's different, and say yes, that was the start of it – that's when it all began, and I didn't even notice. 15

Well, I noticed all right, and it was like – I can't explain. It was like everything shattering apart, y'know? I mean everything. Things I thought I knew. Stuff I'd been taught. The foundation of my life is what I'm talking about here, and I felt it shift, and if you've never felt that then you don't know what I'm talking about. Anyway, it shifted that night and shattered apart and Ma and Pa Askew never got their sweet little Zoe back. Oh, they thought they still had her, but they didn't. It was somebody else. 20 25

Somebody else entirely. *2 parts of Zoe!*

*to contradicts - widersprechen*
*to dare - wagen*
*to confide in - jmd. etw. anvertrauen*

12 **beat-up** (adj, infml): old and damaged    19 **shatter**: suddenly break into small pieces

# DAZ

'Here's Cal now.'

    i lucked, and i seen this littel guy wiv spex. Fin he was. Five foot frag-all wiv blond hair and neat doodies like a Subby. i sez, you jest, and Mick sez no, that's im.

5     i cant beleev it. Like, Cal's a nero, you know? A living ledge end. Peeple tork abowt im all the time. Thers a price on is hed for faxake, and hear he com lucking like a shagged owt det-clecter.

    Aniway he com over and sez somfing 2 Mick and Mick sort of nods at me and nex fing Cal's standing nex 2 me and he sez i'm off
10 4 a slash, foller in a minit. He gos of tord the bog and Mick does a fumsup wiv a silly grin on is face. i wait and wile i'm waiting i shoot anovver glance tord this Subby girl. She's in a corner wiv er mates. She's lucking at me but drops er eyes wen i luck at er. She's making me feal funny and I wish she never com in tonite. Any ovver nite yes
15 but not tonite. Why'd she hafta com in tonite of all nites, screwing me up, like i'm wondering if all Subbys're bad. Cors all Subbys're bad. Evry 1 knows that.

    i go in the bog. Thers 2 guys in, Cal and anovver. i pertend 2 slash and Cal's wiping his hands til the geezer gos. Then he sez strait owt,
20 who's the girl?

    My hart kicks. Wot girl i sez, and he sez i seen you lucking at that Subby tart. Guy fancys Subby tarts no good in Dred. How you feel, sposin you gotta kill er? He torks fast, all the time watching the door. Jumpy i guess. i'd be jumpy an all, 50 thou on my hed.

---

2 **specs** (infml, cf. spectacles [fml]): glasses   2–3 **five foot frag-all** = five foot nothing: *genau fünf Fuß (ca. 1,50 m) groß*   3 **jest** (fml): say things that are not true   5 **a nero** = a hero   6 **for faxake** = for fuck's sake (sl): *Kraftausdruck*
7 **shagged out** [ʃægd] (BE sl): very tired   **det-clecter** = debt collector: *Schuldeneintreiber*   10 **a slash** (BE sl): an act of urinating   **tord**: toward   **bog** (sl): toilet
11 **fumsup** = thumbs up: used to show that sth. has been accepted   19 **geezer** (BE infml): man   22 **tart** (sl): prostitute   24 **jumpy** (infml): nervous   **50 thou**: fifty thousand

i dont know wot 2 say. Panicking inside finking, i'm blowing it. All that time waiting 2 com 15 and now i get my chance i'm blowing it. i kill er, i sez, no danger, but i'm not so shor and i fink he knows it, but before he can say anyfing else thers this crash like some 1 frou somfing and Cal sort ov freezes, lucking at the door. Then he spins 5 rownd and befor i can breeve he's up and away owt the window.

I never seen any 1 move so fast.

# ZOE

We nearly didn't make it. I mean, everything could have ended for 11
the four of us right there in the Blue Moon that night, and it'd all
have been Larry's fault.

 What happened was, he saw this girl. Chippy girl. She was with
5 another girl and two guys and they might have been married for all
we knew but it made no difference to old Larry. She was pretty and
he was smashed and he caught her eye and smiled and started
making signs for her to leave the others and come on over. I felt
quite apprehensive about it in spite of the drink, and so did Ned. He
10 said something to Larry – tried to get him to stop, but Larry accused
him of being jealous and went right on doing it. The girl kept
smiling, but it was the sort of smile people put on when they're
embarrassed and don't know what else to do. I could see that, and
I bet Tabby and Ned could too, but not Larry. Oh no. He thought she
15 fancied him and redoubled his efforts.

 At first the two guys ignored him. Chippies don't like people
from the suburbs and they'd as soon smash a Subby to pulp as not.
But there's always big trouble with the police when something like
that happens, so unless they're members of Dred or very drunk
20 they'll usually bend over backwards not to get involved. In the face
of their seeming indifference, Larry's antics became increasingly
gross, until finally he yelled at the top of his voice, 'Come on over,
honey – you know you're wasted on that trash!' It was just our luck
that this outburst coincided with a break in the music. There was
25 this awful silence while everybody in the room turned to look at us,
and then one of the two guys – the one who was with this girl
I guess – got up and grabbed his chair and came at Larry like he
meant to splatter his brain. He probably would've done it too, if two

---

17 **pulp**: soft wet substance that is made esp. by crushing  21 **indifference**: lack of
interest  **antics**: silly behaviour  22 **gross** [grəʊs]: very rude  23 **just my/sb.'s
luck** (infml): used to show you are not surprised sth. bad has happened to you
24 **coincide** (of two or more events): take place at the same time  28 **splatter sth.**:
*etwas verspritzen*

beefy guys hadn't burst on the scene and put themselves between him and us. They must've been lurking somewhere discreetly, watching the trouble build. When the guy saw he wasn't going to reach Larry he let out a roar and flung the chair. Larry threw up his arms to fend it off, and it bounced off him on to the floor. Meanwhile, 5 the two heavies had grabbed the other guy and were wrestling him towards the door.

Larry was hunched over, moaning and holding his arm. There was still no music, and everybody seemed to be watching us. The atmosphere of resentment was unmistakable: there was a sort of 10 murmur, and I had the distinct feeling that the crowd was closing in on us. I was fuddled with the drink, I guess, but I remember thinking, this is it. We'll never make the door. We're gonna die. Tomorrow they'll find the car, and maybe a shoe.

Then I saw him – the guy I'd been looking at all night. I never 15 saw him arrive, but suddenly there he was and he said, 'You better leave with me. Now.' He didn't pause but sort of walked through us, slipping his arm through Larry's on the way past, helping him along.

We didn't hang around.

1 **beefy** (infml): big or fat    2 **lurk** (v): wait somewhere secretly, esp. because you are going to do sth. bad    5 **fend sb./sth. off**: defend or protect yourself from sb./ sth. that is attacking you    8 **moan** (v): make a long deep sound, usu. expressing unhappiness or suffering    10 **resentment**: feeling of anger or unhappiness about sth. that you think is unfair    12 **fuddled**: unable to think clearly, usu. as a result of drinking alcohol

# DAZ

So this crash com and Cal's away. i open the door a crack and luck 12
owt and its wot i fought. Subbys. i knew ther be trubble tonite wiv
them in. Stanstareeson dunnit.

i luck and i fink, sod em. They blew it 4 me. Let em get topped.
5 Then i seen the girl. The 1 i bin watching. She luck scairt. 2 hunnerd
peeple want me ded, i luck scairt. i seen her and i cant let em do it.
The uvvers i dont give a monkeys abowt but i cant let em top her.

Its a tuff 1 cos the peeples real mad and i gotta be cool. i go over
nice and easy. i tork soft. i tell em you better leave wiv me now, nor
10 I dont stop neever. i grab this fin Subby wots hurting and shov frou
going hello Pete, hows fings Miz Stanton, givin em the big smile.
And all the time i'm finking, we not gonna make it. Somfing gonna
snap but noffing does and it seems a longtime and then were at the
door.

15 i let go the fin Subby. Run, i sez. i know thay gorra motor near.
Thay run. 3 of em. Not her. Run, i sez 2 her. Peeples coming, i sez.
Lucking 2 her, 2 them, 2 her. Fanks, she sez, and she kiss my cheek
quick and runs. i want 2 say somfing back but i dont know wot.
Peeple shoving me. I showt somfing. You nice. i like you. somfing
20 like that, but i dont fink she hears me. A motor starts. Dazzlers com
on, moving. Shes away.

After, i cant beleeve i don it. Wot am i, a Subby or somfing? i got
bags ov time 2 fink about it anall, cos i sure cant go back in the Blew
Moon now. Peeple stairing and muttering.

25 Mick. He give me this luck like i kick him in the teef and then he
turns and gos back in. Evry 1 else gos in 2. i'm on my tod. i luck
arownd 4 Cal but no chance. Black streets. A dog far of. Some rain.
Home then. Watch the box wiv our mam.

---

3 **stanstareeson** = stands to reason: *das leuchtet ein*   4 **sod sb./sth.** (BE sl): forget
sb./th.   7 **not give a monkey's about sb./sth.** (BE sl): not care about sb./sth.
13 **snap**: (here) go wrong   26 **be on your tod** (BE infml): be on your own
28 **the box** (infml): the television

i'm not in Dred, our mam.
That's nice, Daz.
i seen this Subby girl, our mam.
Forget her, Daz.
Not easy, our mam. Not easy.                     5

# ZOE

It must've been the shortest Chippy trip ever. Ned kept his foot 13
down all the way and we were back in Silverdale for nine-thirty.
Nobody spoke to me till Tabby said g'night when they dropped me
off, and it took her all her time to say that. I guess I shouldn't have
5  hung around when it was time to go but the guy had stuck his neck
out for us, hadn't he? I couldn't just run off without saying anything.
Anyway, their being mad at me was the least of my worries right
then. The worst thing was not being able to get the guy out of my
mind. I kept seeing him in that doorway, holding everybody back
10  while we got away. I tried telling myself he was just a Chippy and
Chippies aren't like us and all that sort of stuff, but it was no use.
I knew he was a hero, even if he was a Chippy. He took our part and
he'd suffer for it one way or another.
   And it wasn't only that. If it had been I could have handled it, but
15  there was something else. It was like he'd gotten inside my head and
I couldn't get him out. His smile. I only saw it once across that
crummy room, but it must've printed itself on my eyelids or something because every time I closed them there he was, smiling. I even
saw him when my eyes were open. In fact if you want the truth
20  I wasn't seeing or thinking of anything else.
   When I got in, Dad said 'How was Alice?'
   I had just enough sense left to realise my parents might smell the
booze on me and I was heading straight for my room. 'Fine,' I said.
'Sends her love.' Mum gave me this puzzled look as I breezed by but
25  I didn't stop.
   I made plenty of noise taking off my shoes and brushing my teeth
so they'd think I was going to bed, but I didn't. Not for ages. By a
fantastic coincidence which you won't believe, my window faces
south, and what I did was, I stood for about three hours looking out.

---

5–6 **stick your neck out**: do or say sth. risky    24 **breeze** (v): move in a cheerful
and confident way in a particular direction    28 **coincidence**: *Zufall*

You can't even see the city from my window but I stood there anyway, gazing south and thinking about him.

You don't have to tell me. Crazy, right? I didn't even know his name, but by the time I got into bed one thing had become very clear.                                                                                      5

I had to see him again.

\* \* \*

You have to understand that it was virtually impossible for a sub-urbanite to fraternise with a Chippy. People lived, worked and played inside their own suburb or moved at speed between suburbs, and from newtown to newtown. The only Chippies we saw were   10
those who had passes to come into a suburb to work. They came in the mornings and left at dusk, and they did all the crummiest jobs – digging holes in the road, collecting trash, cleaning washrooms. A few were servants or gardeners in big houses, but they had to leave in the afternoon like the rest. You let a Chippy stay the night, he'll   15
rip off all your stuff and maybe cut your throat for an encore. Chippies're envious, see. Full of hate. Even the lucky ones with jobs in the suburbs. Nobody'd even talk to a Chippy except to tell him what to do, and as kids we'd cross the street whenever we'd see one coming.                                                                                   20

So that was the fix I was in. I couldn't get this guy out of my mind and I had to see him again, but as far as I knew he didn't have a pass, and I certainly couldn't hope to get invited on another chippying expedition for some time. And even if I did, who's to say they'd choose the Blue Moon? And if they did, why should he be there? He   25
might use a different club every night, for all I knew.

---

2 **gaze** (v): look steadily at sb./sth. for a long time    7 **virtually**: almost or very nearly    7–8 **suburbanite**: sb. who lives in a suburb    8 **fraternise with sb.** ['frætənaɪz]: behave in a friendly manner    16 **encore** ['ɒŋkɔ:]: *Zugabe*    21 **fix** (n): (here) difficult situation

I moped. I couldn't eat. Couldn't concentrate. I started avoiding company, and of course Mum noticed the change in me and mentioned it and I damn near bit her head off.

Finally I did what I always did when things got rough for me.
5 I went and talked to Grandma.

* * *

She's one hundred and four years old and she's still got all her marbles. That's not all that unusual in the suburbs, of course. If she'd been a Chippy she'd have been dead fifty years. She's Mum's grandma, not mine, and she sees things differently. I mean, everybody
10 else I know feels more or less the same about most things. I could tell my parents about some problem I was having, or I could talk to one of the teachers at school or I could go to a preacher, and they'd all say the same things, and I'd know all the things they were going to say before they said them. Like, suppose I told about this Chippy
15 guy, right? How I happened to meet him and how I couldn't sleep and all that. Well, it wouldn't matter who I was talking to, they'd start by saying I shouldn't have been chippying in the first place, and then they'd tell me Chippies're not like us – they don't have the same feelings, so it's a mistake to get emotionally involved with one.
20 They'd say that of course any further contact between this guy and me was out of the question, and finish by telling me I wasn't really in love anyway – I was too young. Somewhere along the way they'd probably ask me whose idea it was to go chippying, so my original problem would still be there and I'd have a new one because
25 I refused to give them a name.

So I went to see Grandma. She has an apartment in a senior citizens' block in another part of Silverdale. Wentworth Apartments. I hope I don't need to tell you who put it up. This was a Saturday, by

---

1 **mope**: spend your time doing nothing and feeling sorry for yourself   3 **bite sb.'s head off** (infml): shout at sb., esp. without reason   7 **marbles** (infml): a way of referring to sb.'s intelligence or mental ability

the way, two weeks after the fateful trip. I flashed my ID for the guy on the door, rode the elevator up and rang the bell. I had to wait a bit. Grandma has a quick mind but her legs're slowing down some. She smiled when she opened the door.

'Zoe. How nice.' She peered at me. 'Is something the matter, 5 dear?'

I shrugged and smiled. 'Nothing much, Grandma. I've got to talk to someone, that's all.'

'Then you've picked the right someone.' She's terrific, old Grandma. I mean, if I was a hundred and four I'm sure I'd be too 10 busy wondering how much time I had left and what happens after you die to want to be bothered with other people's problems. Grandma's not like that. She takes the time to listen. Time's the one thing I have, she'll say.

She put me in a chair and fixed coffee like she was the kid and 15 I was the old lady. When it was done she sat down facing me and said, 'Now – what's troubling young Zoe, eh?'

I told her. When I was through she sat for a long time, gazing into her coffee cup. I sipped from mine, thinking, she's stumped. First time ever. She doesn't know what to say to me. 20

Then she started talking, very softly. She didn't look up at me. It was like she was talking to herself. 'I was sixteen,' she said, 'and working in a music shop in Rawhampton city centre. One day a boy came in. A young man, really. Eighteen or nineteen.' She smiled. 'The instant I saw him my heart kicked me so hard in the ribs 25 I couldn't get my breath. I thought I'd die, right there behind the counter. He didn't come to me. I was on records and he wanted a cassette. This friend of mine, Pauline, was on the cassette counter and he went to her. I stood and stared all the time she was attending to him. He was the most gorgeous creature I'd ever seen and 30 I couldn't tear my eyes away. If the boss had come in just then I'd probably have got the sack, but I couldn't help it.' She smiled, lifted

---

1 **fateful**: having an important, often very bad, effect on future events   **flash sth. at sb.** (v): show sth. to sb. quickly   5 **peer** (v): look closely or carefully at sth.
19 **be stumped** (infml): be unable to answer   31 **tear your eyes away** [teə]: look somewhere else   32 **get the sack** (infml): lose your job

her cup and sipped. 'I followed him with my eyes as he left the shop. We didn't have the cassette he wanted and Pauline was ordering it for him. I went across to look at his name on the order pad. I've never forgotten it. It was Gordon Payne, and it rang bells for me.
5 I couldn't understand why Pauline hadn't passed out with excitement, but when I asked her when he was calling in again she said "Tuesday" in a matter-of-fact voice and slid the pad back under the counter.'

'Tuesday.' Grandma sighed. 'Of course, I can't remember now whether it was a Tuesday or some other day. It doesn't matter. The
10 point is, it was four or five days before I saw him again, and during that time I was in torment. I couldn't eat. I couldn't sleep. I mooned all day and neglected my work. I lost interest in my friends and the things I liked to do. I somehow managed to convince myself that he'd noticed me, that he was pining for me right now as I was for
15 him, and that when Tuesday came he'd declare his love and we'd live happily ever after.'

She paused and looked at me. 'He didn't, of course. I'd waited all that morning in what the novelists call an agony of suspense, and when he came in he collected his cassette, paid and left. He hadn't
20 even glanced in my direction and I never saw him again, but it was months before I stopped hoping. Months.'

She sipped her coffee and I said, 'You're warning me, right? You're saying he's probably forgotten me already.'

'I'm saying it's a possibility you should bear in mind, Zoe. It could
25 save you some pain, though of course it'll cause you some, too.' She smiled. 'There was a song – oh, before my time even. "Love Hurts" it was called, and that's what I'm trying to say. It hurts, even when it's got everything going for it. When it hasn't it hurts more, and this love of yours has nothing going for it. Nothing at all.'

30 She meant, with him being a Chippy and all, but she didn't call it impossible or tell me I only thought I was in love, and that's what I mean about Grandma.

---

4 **ring a bell** (infml): sound familiar to you, as though you have heard it before
11 **torment** (n, fml) ['– –]: extreme suffering   **moon** (v): spend time doing nothing or walking around with no particular purpose, esp. because you are unhappy
14 **pine for sb.**: want or miss sb. very much   18 **suspense**: *Ungewissheit*

I nodded. 'I know.' My voice was shaky with trying not to cry. 'But I've got to see him again, Grandma. I've just got to.'

I cried then. I couldn't help it. I slid down off my chair and knelt on the carpet and buried my face in her lap like I used to when I was very small, and she stroked my hair. Neither of us spoke for a while, 5 and then Grandma said, still stroking my hair, 'Wait, Zoe. It's all you can do. If this boy feels anything for you he'll find a way to tell you so. And if he doesn't, you'll be left riding out the pain, as I was.'

It sounded a bleak prospect. I mean, maybe the guy wasn't feeling anything for me right now – he only saw me once, for a few hectic 10 seconds. If we could meet again in different circumstances –.

I sniffled and said, 'Couldn't I go there, Grandma? Back to the Blue Moon?' I felt her shake her head.

'Better not, Zoe. Wait. I know it's hard. It's one of the hardest things there is, but you know we can't make people love us. It 15 happens, or it doesn't. I hope it happens for you, but if it does it'll only be the start of your real worries.' She ruffled my hair and stirred and I lifted my face, leaving a damp place on her skirt. I said, 'I feel much better, Grandma, now I've talked to you.' It was true.

'I feel better too,' she said. 'Perhaps I'm getting over Gordon 20 Payne.'

---

3 **kneel** (**knelt** – **knelt**): be on your knees　8 **ride sth. out**: survive a difficult situation without making great changes　9 **bleak**: not encouraging or giving any reason for hope　**prospect** (n) ['prɒspekt]: the possibility that sth. will happen
12 **sniffle** (v): *schniefen*　17 **ruffle sb.'s hair**: *jdm. die Haare zerzausen*

# DAZ

Mister James sez Wots got in 2 you Darren? He calls me Darren. its a
fursday and i'm in school. i dint jack it in cos i'm not in Dred. Well
its som wear to go innit.

Noffing sir i sez, but thats a fib. somfing got in 2 me alrite and
5  i know wot. Subby girl got in 2 me but i cant tell him that, can i?

It screwed evryfing up, that nite. Evryfing. i wish it never happen
but it did. i cant stop finking abowt her, even thogh i know she dont
give a monkeys abowt me. Subbys dont fink we human even, but
i fink abowt her all the time. How she hung abowt 2 say fanks. Kiss
10  me. Gotta mean somfing, rite?

Rong. Dont mean noffing. Subby trash playing arownd, like thay
do. i wish i never helpt em. i do. Mick stopt coming 2 school. He's in
Dred. Only com 2 school cos i do and now hes gon. Week after that
nite i call rownd his place. Arst him 2 fix anovver meeting wiv Cal.
15  Yor joking, he sez. Cal risk his life 4 you and wot dos he see – he sees
a guying lucking at Subbys like he lovs em. Sees a guy sooner help
Subbys than his own sort. Own famly, mebbe. You make a prat outa
me Daz, he sez, and nobody makes a prat outa me. Bog off he sez,
and dont you com rownd no more.

20  i want 2 join Dred. i do, but i keep seeing Cal. Jumpy Cal. The
luck in his eyes. The way he went frou that window.

So evryfings mucked up, rite? Only 1 happy our mam and she
dont know abowt the girl. If she did she wont be 2 happy neever
I can tell you.

25  Aniway thats wots got in 2 Darren Mister James.
Noffing.

4 **fib** (n): lie   18 **prat** (sl): stupid person   **bog off**!: (BE sl): go away!   22 **muck
sth. up** (infml): mess sth. up

# ZOE

**15** I really did feel better after I talked to Grandma. I'd been hatching all
sorts of wild plans aimed at getting back to the Blue Moon, torturing
myself with pictures of him finding someone, telling myself I could
be that someone if only I wasn't trapped in a cage called Silverdale.
Now I found I had the strength to shut out these thoughts, and it    5
was one less thing to fret about. It's out of my hands, I told myself.
I can only wait. It was sort of restful for a while.

I'm not saying it was easy. It wasn't. Waiting for something you
really, really want and probably won't get is terrible, and it's particularly bad if you can't share it with those around you. I mean I couldn't    10
say to my parents, oh by the way if you find me a little tense these
days don't worry. I'm expecting a message from this Chippy guy
I met, or maybe even a midnight visit, and if it happens we just
might go off together. I couldn't tell them I was under a strain, and
so I had to try to be my old sweet self, answering politely when they    15
asked about school and friends and things like that – stuff I didn't
care about anymore. It affected me in various unexpected ways.

Like that same Saturday. That day, while I was visiting with
Grandma there'd been some sort of disturbance in the city. A riot. It
happens a lot, and there's usually a bit on the news about it, and    20
then Dad will have something to say about Chippies and what he'd
do to them if he were the government. He always says the same
things, and I don't pay it any heed because it's just an automatic
response with him and it's not important, anyway – he's never going
to be the government. Mum doesn't pay it any heed either – maybe    25
she doesn't even hear it anymore. Anyway, this item comes on screen
and Dad says 'Riot? I'd give 'em riot. I'd have a door-gunner in every

---

1 **hatch sth.**: create a plan or idea, esp. in secret    6 **fret about sth.**: worry about
sth.    14 **be under a strain**: be under pressure    17 **affect sb./sth.**: have an
influence on sb./sth.    19 **disturbance**: *Störung*    23 **pay heed to sth.**: pay attention
to sth.

'copter and cream 'em.' He snorts. 'They'd think twice before they'd riot again, I can tell you.'

As I say, he'd said it all before, only this time I got a picture of Chippies crumpling under a hail of lead, and one of them was you
5 know who. I said, 'They're people, Dad. Some of them're probably nice if you know them.'

He looked at me sharply, then his startled expression softened into a sneer. 'Nice? I'll tell you how nice they are, Zoe. One night a couple of months ago a bunch of Fairlawn kids drove into the city.
10 Their folks thought they were visiting Goldengrove, and when they hadn't returned at midnight a parent raised the alarm.' He paused to create some suspense. 'They found them next day, four of 'em, hanging by their feet on the forecourt of a derelict gas station, shot through the back of the neck.'

15 Mum said 'Gerald!' – like that. I guess she thought Dad ought not to have told me this horrible story but it was all right. I'd heard it ages ago from Tabby, who likes such things. I said 'That was Dred, Dad. They're not all in Dred. Most of them're just poor folks getting along the best way they can.'

20 'Oh yeah?' I could see he was getting mad but I was mad too. 'And just what in the bright blue blazes d'you think you know about it, Zoe? You, who've never so much as set foot outside of Silverdale in the whole of your spoiled little life?'

I wanted to tell him then. Oh, I did. About the trash and the dogs
25 and the Blue Moon and Chippy eyes up close. The crowd closing in and the way we were saved. I wanted to see the look on his face but of course I couldn't so I said, 'Grandma says they're people like you and me.'

'Grandma's an old lady,' he said. 'Her savvy's out to lunch.'

---

1 **'copter** = helicopter   **cream sb.**: completely defeat sb.   **snort** (v): make a loud sound by breathing air out noisily to show that you are angry   4 **crumple**: collapse **hail of lead**: *Kugelhagel*   7 **startled**: surprised   8 **sneer**: unpleasant look, smile or comment that shows you do not respect sb.   13 **forecourt**: large open space in front of a building   21 **what in the bright blue blazes …?**: *Was zum Teufel …?* 23 **spoiled**: *verwöhnt*   29 **savvy** (infml): practical knowledge of sth.   **out to lunch** (infml): behaving in a strange way

Mum shot him a look because this was vulgar and also untrue.
I didn't say anything. I got up and walked out and went to my room
and drew a helicopter and wrote 'FAN' underneath in big letters and
left it around for him to find. Fan's a Chippy word and he hates me
using Chippy words.                                                    5

* * *

So I was in trouble at home. This was on top of my original problem,
plus the fact that my few friends were cooling off from neglect and
I couldn't get interested in anything.
    Then, just as it began to seem that nothing would ever be right
again, something else went wrong.                                     10
    I got in trouble at school, and this was something new for me.
I believe in keeping my head down so I don't get noticed, and this
has usually worked. I never got detentions or counselling or any of
that stuff. Not until this day I'm going to tell about.
    It was a Monday – the Monday after my Saturday clash with Dad.   15
Modern History with Miss Moncrieff. I've never liked old Moncrieff
and I usually switch off in her class because history's so boring.
Dates, dust and dead men, right?
    Anyway, it was Modern History and I was looking out of the
window. It was one of those gorgeous mornings you sometimes get      20
in October when the sun shines through mist and makes it look like
gold, and the dew's still on the grass and that's gold too, and all the
trees are red and gold and there are spider webs made of crystal lace.
I was looking out the window, wishing I was out there walking hand
in hand with you know who, and Moncrieff's voice was droning on      25
in the background. She was talking about something called the

7 **neglect** (n): the fact of not giving enough care or attention to sb.    13 **detention**:
the punishment of being kept at school after all other students have gone home
**counselling**: professional advice about a problem    15 **clash**: fight    21 **mist**: *Nebel*
22 **dew**: very small drops of water that form e.g. on the ground during the night
23 **lace**: delicate material made from threads of cotton, silk, etc. (*Spitze*)

*Bähnen !*

Franchise (Income Qualification) Bill of 2004. (Yawn, yawn.) Not the most riveting stuff, even the first time around, and this was the second time around because we were revising for the November exams. Well – the others were. I was rehearsing something else
5   entirely.

Anyway she's on about this bill and she must've spotted that I wasn't paying attention and she stops droning and goes, 'Why did the Dennison government introduce this bill, Zoe Askew?'

'What bill, Miss?' I asked. Well, she took me by surprise.
10   'The bill I've been talking about for the last half hour while you've been gazing out the window.'

'I don't know, Miss.'

You could tell she didn't like it. She grew very still. Her cheeks went white and twitched a couple of times as she looked at me. I felt
15   quite nervous. I thought she might flip and fling herself at me, screaming.

She didn't. Instead she started speaking, softly and very distinctly, moving her mouth in an exaggerated way like I was just learning to lip-read or something. 'The Franchise (Income Qualification) Bill
20   was introduced to correct an anomaly whereby those sections of the population which contributed least to society were able to exercise undue influence upon it through misuse of the vote.' She looked at me. 'Do you think you can remember that?'

'Yes, Miss.'
25   'Good.' She smiled like a shark. 'Because when you go home this afternoon you will write it out forty-five times, word for word in your neatest hand – that's one time for each minute you've wasted in my class today.'

---

1 **franchise**: (fml) the right to vote in a country's elections   **yawn**: open your mouth
and breathe because you are tired   2 **rivet** (v): hold sb.'s interest or attention
4 **rehearse** [rɪhɜːs]: practise sth. in preparation for a performance   14 **twitch** (of
parts of the body): make a sudden quick movement   15 **flip** (v, infml): become
very angry   **fling** (flung – flung) **sb./sth. at sb./sth.**: throw sb./sth. at sth.
18 **exaggerated**: *übertrieben*   20 **anomaly** [ə'nɒməli]: thing, situation, etc. that is
different from what is normal or expected   21 **contribute to sth.**: give sth., esp.
money   22 **undue** (fml) [ˌʌn'djuː]: unreasonable or unnecessary   **misuse**:
*Missbrauch*   25 **shark**: *Hai*

Some of the kids tittered and she froze them with her gorgon special. That's a look she gives which damn near turns you to stone. She thought they were laughing at me but they weren't. I knew why they were laughing. They were thinking, we've all wasted the forty-five minutes, Miss – that's what your classes are – a waste of time, 5 but of course nobody would say it. I was the only one dumb enough to talk back to old Moncrieff.

I know what you're thinking. You're thinking, is that it? Is that what you call trouble – a few stupid lines to write out?

Well, no it isn't. We haven't got to the trouble yet. That's coming 10 up next, as they say on telly.

1 **gorgon** (in ancient Greek stories): one of three sisters with snakes for hair who changed anyone that looked at them into stone

# DAZ

Dred gud, Subbys bad
Dred gud, Subbys bad
Dred gud, Subbys bad
Dred gud, Subbys bad
5   Dred gud, Subbys bad
Dred gud, Subbys bad
Dred gud, Subbys bad

*brain washing himself to forgett Zoe*

16

i rite this all down my maffs book.

Mister James sez, you spose to be doing maffs.

10   Wot's a maff, i sez, so he frow me owt, nor I can't go back no more.

Subbys call it Chippy grad you ayshon.

---

12 **grad you ayshon** = graduation: act of successfully completing school or university

# ZOE

**17**   I did it. I wrote it out forty-five times in my neatest hand and it took all evening. It was a drag all right, but when Moncrieff tells you to do something it's best to do it.

I did it, and then I sat looking at it for a long time in the light from my desktop lamp. I'd filled thirteen sheets of paper. Thirteen, and I knew exactly what she'd do when I handed them to her because I'd seen her do it to other kids. She wouldn't read them. She'd riffle through to make sure I hadn't slipped in any blanks. If all the sheets were filled and the whole thing looked neat she'd tear it in half and dump it in her wastepaper basket. Three hours to produce, three seconds to dispose of. Part of the punishment, right? If she found sloppy work or blanks she'd have me do the whole thing again.

Anyway, I sat looking at it, and then I pulled the last sheet towards me and scrawled 'Brainwashing' across the bottom. I don't know if you're familiar with that term. Brainwashing. I am, because Grandma uses it all the time. She says half of what's on TV and in the papers is brainwashing, and she reckons a lot of what they teach us in school is brainwashing too. When I asked her what brainwashing is, she told me it's repeating lies over and over till people come to believe them. She says Dad's the most brainwashed person she ever met. I looked at what Moncrieff had made me write and I thought, this is brainwashing. What the Dennison government did was take the vote away from the Chippies, and what I've just written out forty-five times is the excuse they gave for doing it. Repeating lies over and over till –.

Well, it hadn't worked with Grandma, and it wasn't going to work with me, and that's why I wrote 'Brainwashing' across the last sheet. I'd like to claim I did it for old Moncrieff, but I didn't. Like

---

8 **blank** (n): empty space   11 **dispose of sth.**: get rid of sth. that you do not want
12 **sloppy**: not neat and tidy   15 **scrawl**: write sth. in a careless, untidy way

I said, she never reads kids' lines, so I knew she'd never see it. It was a gesture, I guess. Just a gesture. Trouble is, Moncrieff chose that Tuesday morning to break the habit of a lifetime.

2 **gesture**: sth. that you do or say to show a particular feeling   3 **habit**: sth. that you do regularly or usually, often without thinking about it because you have done it so many times before

# DAZ

**18** Wen you fink abowt some 1 all the time and you cant see them its bad. Wen you gat noffing els 2 do its worse. I got noffing els 2 do now.

1 day i'm sitting in the flat finking as usual and i remember somfing this guy Clint shown me longtime back. Clint you basted you ded 2 years now and serve you rite. This Clint hes in Dred wiv our Del rite? Hes in Dred but i dont know why thay want him. Hes got a big mouf, Clint. Aster let peeple know wot hes doing all the time. Aster be a nero.

Aniway its him wot gets our Del topped. Him and his big mouf. They done a job togevver see, only the nite before, this Clint he gets drunk and blabs and some 1 over ears him – lornorder mebbe, or a Subby. No 1 knows, but thay waiting and thay get our Del and Clint gets away, nor Del dont split on him neever. But after thay top him this Clint vanishes and no 1 ever sees him again. Evry 1 knows Dred fixt him but no 1 torking abowt it. Any 1 tork Dred biznis gotta be crazy, rite?

Aniway this 1 time – i'm 11 i fink, Clint shown me how Dred get into Silverdale. That's the sort of guy he was – hed show somfing like that to a littel kid. We're way up in the norf part of the city seeing wat we can find, and he luck norf and smile and sez, Silverdale that way. i can go in ther anitime.

o no you cant i sez. i know he got no seeit. No veeza. you cant get in Silverdale any more'n i can, I sez.

o yes I can, he sez. Dred way, see?

Wots that, i sez. Dred way?

5 **bastard** (n, sl): used to insult sb. *(jdn. beschimpfen)* who has been cruel   12 **blab** (infml): tell sb. sth. that should be kept secret   12 **over ear** = overhear: hear sth. others say by accident   14 **split on sb.** (BE infml): tell sb. in authority about sth. wrong that sb. else has done   15 **vanish**: disappear suddenly   16 **fix sb.** (infml): punish sb. and stop them doing any more harm   **biznis** = business   23 **see-it**: identification papers

He shown me. Thers like this big lid rite? In the road. Big iron lid, and Clint he lift it up and thers a hoal wiv a ladder going down and he sez, see that? Thers a tunnel down there wot goes rite inter Silverdale. i dont beleeve him. if it goes inter Silverdale I sez, how
5   come evry 1 dont go? How come guys cut the fence and the dazzlers catch em and they get shot?

he larfs. its not just 1 tunnel he sez. its lots of tunnels. You gotta know the way see, or you mite get lost. Wander in the dark til you die. Aniway he sez, any 1 else go in there, Dred top em.
10   i remember this wot Clint shown me all those years back and i fink well im going frou, Dred or no Dred. When you gotta see some 1, you gotta see em.

i start 2 make a plan.

---

1 **lid**: cover for the open part of a container or hole

# ZOE

19  Tuesday morning, breaktime. I take my thirteen sheets along to the
staffroom and knock. Moncrieff answers the door herself. She has
this bright, enquiring look on her mug but when she sees who it is
her features sort of shift around till she's looking at me like I'm a dog
turd.                                                                                    5

'Yes?'

'Lines, Miss.' I hold out the wad.

'Hmm.' She takes them. I stand looking bored while she riffles
through. I'm not going to flinch when she rips them up. I won't even
blink. I'll keep this blank expression so she'll know I don't give a          10
toss.

'What's this?'

I focus my eyes. 'Huh?'

'This.' She's waving the thirteenth sheet in my face.

'Brainwashing. What d'you mean by it, eh?'                                        15

My heart gives a painful lurch and I swallow hard. For the first
time in living memory she actually looks at a set of lines and it has to
be mine. Act cool, Zoe kid – it's your only chance. I frown at the
paper like I'm seeing it for the first time and I say, 'I dunno, Miss. I
guess that must've been there before I wrote the lines.'                          20

She sneers. 'Do you expect me to believe that, Askew?' Askew. It's
been Zoe ever since I've been at this school and now it's Askew. This
gets me mad. Don't ask me why because I don't know. Like I said
before, I'm not the sort of kid who gets in trouble at school. I don't
get mad at teachers, I get scared. I guess it must be all this other stuff   25
that's been building up without my realising it. Anyway, whatever it
is I'm blazing mad and I hear myself say, 'I don't give a monkey's
what you think, Moncrieff.'

---

3 **enquiring**: asking for information   **mug** (sl): person's face   5 **turd** (sl): *Kot*
9 **flinch**: *zucken*   10–11 **not give a toss** (BE sl): not care at all   16 **lurch** (n):
sudden strong movement   **swallow**: *schlucken*   18 **frown**: *die Stirn runzeln*

It wasn't me. That's all I can say. It just wasn't me.

I won't go into all the stuff that went down after I said what I said, but it ended with Moncrieff writing a note to my parents and me taking it home. I say ended, but of course it didn't end there.

# DAZ

**20**    i make this plan rite, and strait off i hit a snag. 2 snags.

1. wot if she dont live in Silverdale.
2. even if she does i dunno witch part.

well i can get in Silverdale. i cant get in aniwear else. So. i go inter
Silverdale and luck 4 her dont i? if she dont live ther 2 bad.    5
witch part thogh? i dunno. fousands ov howses in Silverdale. cud
be any ov them. and if i find it, wot do i do eh – nock on the door?
O yeah i can just seeit. Hello mister Subby i come for your littel girl.
O rite i'll get her 4 you. wot you do wiv her by the way?
O we run of togevver. liv in the city. you never see her again.    10
O well thats alrite then.
O.K. so i dont go 2 her howse. Shes yung rite? still at school.
fousands ov howses. Not fowsands ov schools. So. i luck 4 schools
not schools 4 tiny littel Subbys neever. schools 4 big kids. cant be
many ov them in Silverdale. 2, if that many. maybe just 1. So i'm not    15
just a pretty face am i?
our mam says that.
nex fing – time. see – i fink ov evryfing. No use getting ther and
all the kids inside. so 2 chances

1. get ther first – watch kids go in.    20
2. end ov day – watch them leev. thats better cos not 2 long til
dark.

i'm riting this plan down. Mister James be prowd ov me.
so here it is. i go frou the tunnel get in Silverdale near sundown.
Pertend i got graft there. Find big kids school. hang abowt. if i see    25
her grate. if not tuff.

---

1 **snag** (infml): problem or difficulty    25 **pertend** = pretend    26 **tuff** = tough

only 1 more fing – wen? Tonite? no. not enuff time. Gotta take it easy see. fink wot doodies 2 wear. wot 2 take wiv me. stuff like that. You rush inter fings, end up ded. Speshly in tunnels.

3 **speshly** = especially

# ZOE

**21**  'What's come over her, Amanda, that's what I'd like to know.'

'God only knows, Gerald. I'm sure I don't.'

This is my parents talking, right? Amanda and Gerald. They're talking about me. I'm there, but they're talking as if I'm not. It's tea-time. I've just delivered Moncrieff's note and they've taken turns 5 reading it. I'm the only one who doesn't know what she's put. Dad's in the easy chair and Mum's perched on the arm and I stand on the rug in front of them with my hands behind my back, looking at the floor and shifting my weight from one foot to the other. It's embarrassing. 10

'First she contradicts me to give us the benefit of her opinion on Chippies, then she mopes and sulks for weeks on end till we're frantic with worry, and now this.' He waves the note at me. 'What's going on, Zoe, eh? What's happening to you? D'you want to drive your mother and me crazy or what?' 15

'May I read the note?' I hold out my hand but he shakes his head and says, 'Never mind the note. You know what prompted Miss Moncrieff to write it so you must have a fair idea what it says. Why did you scrawl "brainwashing" across the lines she gave you?'

'Why did you have to write them in the first place?' This from 20 Mum. 'What were you doing wrong, Zoe?'

I shrugged. 'She gave me lines for looking out the window.' I considered telling about the misty sunlight and the spider webs and all but it would've been a waste of breath. I said, 'What she made me write is a lie.' 25

Dad's eyebrows went up. 'Oh, really? What was it exactly?'

I told him and he said 'Who told you it was a lie? Who's been talking to you, Zoe – your grandma?' He's got a thing about Grandma. Thinks she's a bad influence. Once when he was real mad he called her a communist and that caused a fight between Mum and him. 30

---

7 **perch** (v, infml): sit on (the edge of) sth.    8 **rug**: small carpet    12 **sulk** (v): *schmollen*    24 **a waste of breath**: useless

I shook my head. 'Nobody talked to me, Dad. I thought it out. They took the vote away from the Chippies and they knew it was wrong so they made up an excuse and I had to write it out forty-five times and that's brainwashing.'

5   'Nonsense!' He leaned forward in the chair. 'Now listen here, young woman: I've had it just about up to here with your recent behaviour, and so has your mother. I don't know what triggered it off, but whatever it was it stops – right here, right now.' He stood up, thrusting the note in his pocket. 'Tomorrow morning before your

10  first class, you'll apologise to Miss Moncrieff for having defaced the work she set you, and in the meantime you'll write out those forty-five lines again, for me. And I don't want to find any smart footnotes either. Is that clear?'

It was, and I did it, and it took till nine thirty. I spent from then

15  till about ten-thirty at my window, gazing south. It was raining. Finally I got into bed and lay thinking about how it'd be, apologizing to old Moncrieff.

Maybe I'll kill myself instead.

* * *

I didn't kill myself or I wouldn't be writing this, would I? Oh, I

20  thought about it. I thought about it for quite a while that night: how I'd leave a note for my parents, forgiving them for their unjust treatment of me. When I failed to appear at breakfast Mum would call, and when I still didn't show up she'd come to my room and there I'd be, pale and cold and very still, but smiling so sweetly that

25  all who beheld me would be struck at once with a sense of my total blamelessness. And then they'd find the note on the bedside unit and read it and boy, would they be sorry. How they'd weep. How they'd wish it could be yesterday again so they could have another

---

1 **think sth. out**: consider or plan sth. carefully   7–8 **trigger sth. off**: cause sth.
10 **apologise to sb.**: say that you are sorry   **deface sth.**: damage the appearance of
sth. esp. by drawing or writing on it   24 **pale**: white in the face   25 **behold sb.**
(fml): look at or see sb.   26 **blamelessness**: *Unschuld*   27 **weep** (fml): cry

chance with me. They'd call me that poor, misunderstood lamb and all like that, but it'd be too late, wouldn't it? I'd be gone, and all the sorrow and repentance in the world wouldn't bring me back.

And that's the snag, right? Because I wouldn't get to see any of this. I wouldn't even know about it. I mean, it'd be fine and dandy 5 if I was going to be sitting somewhere out of sight, looking on. Watching the devastation my simple act had wrought, but I wouldn't be, would I? Dead is dead, and there's no satisfaction in revenge if you're not around to enjoy it.

So I stayed alive and apologized to Moncrieff. Oh, how could 10 you, I hear you cry. How did you stand it – the humiliation and all?

Well, I'll tell you in a single word. Galileo.

Let me explain.

Galileo was the guy who invented the telescope, and when he'd invented it he used it to look at the moon and the stars and the 15 planets and all that, and he made a startling discovery. He discovered that the earth didn't stand still like people thought in those days, with the sun and moon and stars going round and round for our especial benefit. No. He saw that it was the earth that moved, round and round the sun. This was a very revolutionary discovery, and 20 Galileo wrote it down so others could share his knowledge.

And that was his big mistake, because the guys in charge back then didn't like his discovery. They wanted everybody to go on believing that the earth was in the middle with everything else going round it. So they sent for Galileo and they said it's not true, what 25 you're saying. It's all lies. And Galileo said no it's not, it's true, and if you don't believe me take a peek through my telescope.

They wouldn't do it, though. They didn't want to know. They said, we want you to say you were mistaken. We want you to tell everybody that. In fact, we command you to. But Galileo shook his 30 head and said, I can't tell 'em that. I'm not mistaken – you are.

---

3 **repentance**: fact of showing that you are sorry for sth. wrong that you have done
5 **dandy** (adj): very good    7 **devastation**: extreme shock    **wreak (wrought –
wrought) sth. on sb./sth.** (fml) [ri:k]: do great damage or harm to sb./sth.
11 **humiliation**: *Erniedrigung*    16 **discovery**: act of finding out sth. new
19 **benefit** (n): helpful and useful effect of sth.    27 **peek** (n): a quick look

And this is where they really got mad. They said, you don't understand. Either you tell everybody you were wrong, or we burn you alive.

Well, now that they'd explained it more clearly Galileo told
5  everybody he'd made a mistake. He said his idea of the universe was wrong, but it was just words, right? He knew all the time he was right, only he said the words they wanted to hear so they wouldn't burn him.

And that's how I apologised to old Moncrieff. I said some words
10  to her so they wouldn't kick me out of school, but I knew all the time me and Grandma were right about brainwashing.

Hang in there, Galileo. Way to go, man!

---

12 **hang in there** (infml): *Halte durch!*   **way to go**: used to tell sb. that you are pleased about sth. they have done

# DAZ

Fursday afternoon i smuggel my stuff owt the flat wile our mam up
the helf. She's down wiv the dulleye as usual and gon for her scrip.
i got these coveralls you gotta wear in Veezaville.

Blue wiv a big yeller disc so they know yor a Chippy. i got the
cap 2. Blue baseball cap. i gotta flashlite and a big ball ov twine.　5

Cost me all my peanuts but i gotta do it, rite? I wisht I gotta seeit
anall but they cost moren i got plus not easy to contact the deela.

i know wot you finking. You finking wots he want wiv twine
encha? Well, i tell you. 1 time up the school Mister James tel this
story abowt sum guy wayback after go frou this maze. Maze is lots of　10
tunnels like i after go frou. This guy scairt he get lost in this maze,
plus its got this monster in it – this miner tour. So wot he does is he
has his ball ov twine witch he lets it owt as he goes frou so he can
foller it back and if he can i can, see?

Aniway I get all this stuff in a plastic sac and i go norf and luck　15
arownd til i find the lid in the road. 2 many people so i pertend i'm
jus passing til thay gon. Then i lift the lid and luck in the hoal. Black
hoal. i feel funny lucking down plus it stinks. Troof is, now i'm here
i dont feal 2 good abowt going down. i tel myself i dont afta but then
i fink ov her and here i go.　20

its not easy standing on this fin rusty ladder wiv my sac and I
gorra put the lid on fore any 1 coms. i luck down but cant see the
bottom. Drop the sac, i sez 2 myself. Take a chance. if it lands in
water 2 bad. i drop it and hear a fud so thats okay. i nearly fal off the
ladder shifting the lid but i get it on nor i dont fink any 1 seen me　25
neeva but its reely dark and stinky and i'm scairt. i go down the
ladder, bits ov it come off on my hands and fall on my hed and 1 bit

---

2 **up the helf**: at the doctor's　**scrip** = prescription: Rezept (vom Arzt)　3 **coveralls**
(AE) = overalls (BE)　5 **twine**: *Schnur*　7 **moren** = more than　9 **encha** = ain't
you = aren't you　10 **after** = have to　**maze**: kind of labyrinth　12 **miner tour** =
Minotaur ['maɪnətɔː]: in ancient Greek stories an imaginary creature who was half
man and half bull

goes in my mouf and when i spit it makes like a lowd ekco noise and
i wisht i never done it.

Longway to the bottom but i make it. Standing in somfing soft
and wet. Feel about 4 the sac, finking i hope that flashlite okay. if the
5  drop smasht it i'm not going. No way. i find it and it lites fank god.
i shine it about. All bricks wiv wite stuff like wool or spiderweb
hanging down. 1 tunnel leading of. Just 1, fank god again. if i seen
2 tunnels i wunt know witch, rite?

its cold. My breff is so lowd i wisht i didn't afta breeve. Water
10  dripping 2 so plenty ov ekco. i keep finking about that miner tour
and i dont want to leeve the ladder. Dont tork so daft i sez, only i say
it in my hed so no ekco. That Clint go frou, any 1 can. This dont
make me feel better cos now i fink abowt Clint goast. No such fing i
tel myself but still scairt and not even started yet.

15  Get a grip i sez inside my hed. Do somfing take yor mind of it ha
ha. So i put the flashlite in my teef and get the twine and tie 1 end to
the ladder and the flashlite all the time jerking abowt making funny
shadders on the bricks only not 2 funny rite? Aniway doing somfing
makes me feel better. i tie the sac frou my belt so boaf hands free and
20  i can hold the flashlite in 1 hand and the twine in the ovver. if i stop
to fink i be up that ladder like a rat up a shitpipe so i dont. i say help
me god and i'm in the tunnel going norf.

i hope.

---

21 **shitpipe** (sl): *Abwasserrohr*

# ZOE

23   So I didn't get kicked out of school but that doesn't mean everything
was okay. Far from it. There's a name they call people who fraternise
with Chippies – those who get too pally with the hired help or fix
coffee for the guys on the garbage truck or something. Chippy-lover.
That's what they call 'em. Now you might think the more love there    5
is around the better, but Chippy-lover's a deadly insult. Folks start
calling you that, you're liable to lose friends because the friend of a
Chippy-lover is a Chippy-lover, if you see what I mean. And that's
what some of the kids called me that day, right after I did my Galileo
riff with old Moncrieff. I guess they thought I was sticking up for    10
Chippy rights over the vote thing, and they were right. What they
didn't know was why. Not that it'd have made things any better for
me if they had. If they'd known little Zoe was totally gone on some
flaky guy with long hair and a leather jacket, little Zoe would
probably have had to quit school right then and there for her own    15
safety. As it was, it must've looked to them like I'd gone soft on
Chippies just to be different or something, and some of them called
after me in the yard and then along the street.

I tried to act like it didn't bother me, but it did. I had so few
friends I couldn't afford enemies. I hurried off up the street, trying    20
not to look like someone in a hurry and wondering what would
happen later when I called for Tabby. Wednesday nights Tabby and
me go to youth club, and I pictured myself walking up to her door
as usual and ringing the bell, only this time Mrs Wentworth answers
it and when she sees it's me she looks down her nose and says, I'm    25
sorry dear, Tabitha won't be joining you this evening, and I can tell
from the way she says it that Tabitha won't be joining me any other
time either from now on, because she's a Wentworth and Wentworths
don't associate with Chippy-lovers.

---

3 **be pally with sb.**: be friendly with sb.    10 **riff**: (here) stunt    13 **be gone on sb.**:
be in love with sb.    14 **flaky** (infml): behaving in a strange or unusual way
16 **go soft on sb./sth.**: become mild, tolerant with sb.

What I did was, I went a long way round to shake off my tormentors, walking rapidly through drifts of fallen leaves, towards the waste ground just inside the boundary fence where nobody ever goes except cats and little kids, and I never did find out what would
5   have happened at Tabby's place that night, because something happened out there. Something staggering.

2 **tormentor** (fml) [–'– –]: person who causes sb. to suffer   3 **waste ground**: area of open land   6 **staggering**: shocking, surprising

# DAZ

24  if you fink i'm wadin frou Subby muck you rong. This tunnel old
rite? It was here before Silverdale and no 1 use it no more. Most old
tunnels blockt of but sum 1 forgot this 1.

So. No Subby muck. Just rat muck plus rats. i hear em and i seen
ther littel eyes. Thay dont bovver me, the rats. Thay reel, like me.      5
Not like that miner tour and Clint goast and moving shadders. Not
like the ekco neever. Give me the rats ennitime.

Aniway i'm up this tunnel and evryfing going slow exept my hart,
witch is going pretty fast. i'm shining the flashlite on the flor and
sides and top, mostly flor, and letting out the twine. Wite stuff      10
hanging down evriwear gets in my hair i dunno wot it is. Miner tour
fur, mebbe. its cold like ice down here, but i'm getting use 2 the
stink – dont notis it no more. i make so much noise walking and
breeving it sownds like thers sum 1 follering but only drippy ekco
wen i stop. i'm going on like this, stopping and starting, scairt, but      15
saying easy-peasy, not long now, wen suddenly thers 2 tunnels.

i stop, but my hart speeds up sum more. Dont panic, i sez. Fink.
i stand ther wiv these 2 black hoals in front ov me, finking, but it
dont do no good. no marks aniwear. no way 2 tel witch way Silverdale. Boaf ways mebbe. Or non. So its a tossup only i got nuffing to      20
toss so i try rite. i remember wot Clint sez abowt gerrin lost down
here til i die, and a few steps in i stop 2 check my twine. its okay.

This tunnel difrent thogh. hoals both sides leeding of, and pretty
soon it splits again and i after chooz. i fink, if i go rite again i'm
gonna sail rite past Silverdale. i go left and i check my twine again.      25
You in a stinky black maze, you check yor twine an all i bet.

Aniway by this time i'm starting 2 wonder does this tunnel reely
go 2 Silverdale or was that Clint winding me up. Mebbe this tunnel
goes nowear. Mebbe it goes 2 the sea. i seen the sea 1 time. its big.
And wile i'm wondering this i see somfing on the flor in frunt ov me.      30

---

5 **thay reel** = they are real    12 **fur**: hair on the body of an animal    20 **toss-up**:
situation in which either of two choices is equally possible

somfing wite and its not hanging down neever. i moov tord it slow, shining the flashlite on it and wen i see wot it is i yell out and my yell ekco and ekco and i neerly turn and run.

its a skelington.

5     this skelington mouf open like it larfing only noffing much to larf abowt rite? Bits of old doodies on it and legboans stuck in dockmartins. i shine my flashlite over it and then i seen somfing make me glad. i know wot you finking. you finking cant be noffing make me glad near a skelington but you rong. Ded rong. (ha ha geddit?) this
10 skelington on its armboan got this band. plastic armband wiv D on it and this is not D for ded this is D for Dred. this wots left ov 1 Dred and i fink, he been 2 Silverdale i bet. got hit not kilt rite away. tryd 2 get hoam but died here. So. i'm going the rite way rite?

littel voyce in my head sez mebbe not. Mebbe this guy lost like
15 you. Shut yor mouf i sez. Wot you wanta go scair me for eh? i stept over the rags and boans and went on kwick.

i'm scairt alrite but noffing else happened plus no more splits in the tunnel. My ball ov twine getting littel thogh, and just wen i fink mebbe it run owt i see lite ahead.

20     i head 4 the lite, mooving reel slow, finking, Silverdale owt ther boy. You get cort now, you ded. i creep up 2 the end and luck owt. its been longer than i fought gerrin here. Daylite nearly gon but i see why this tunnel aint blockt of. it coms owt a little hilside. Piles ov muck all rownd. Erf and stoans and smasht up brix and long grass
25 over it like sumplace in the city. i never new they had places like this in Veezaville. 1 pile ov muck rite in frunt ov the tunnel plus fireweed and littel trees. hundreds peeple pass by, no 1 see this hoal.

i go back in, strip off my doodies, get into coveralls and cap. now I'm a Chippy wiv graft in Silverdale. i put my doodies in the sac and
30 hide it in the tunnel. i put the littel ball ov twine on the flor wiv a stoan on top. Then i walk out the hoal and frou the piles ov muck like i done it evry day. Gotta luck cool or sum bouncer ast 4 my seeit and i aint got 1. i'm just finking wear the big kid school wen somfing

---

4 **skelington** = skeleton    9 **ded rong** = dead wrong (infml): completely wrong
24 **muck**: dirt    26 **fireweed**: *Weidenröschen*

umbeleevabel happens. i luck rownd and ther she is – the girl I come 4.

troof is stronger than friction, rite?

3 **troof is stronger than friction**: cf. saying: truth is stranger than fiction

# ZOE

It was like Grandma when Gordon Payne walked in that music shop.
My heart kicked and I forgot how to breathe and my legs practically
gave way under me. Only thing that went on working was my mind,
and that must've gone into overdrive because in the second between
5 me seeing him and him seeing me it processed about fifty thousand
thoughts.

First I thought, it's not him. It's some guy who looks like him. It
was almost dark, see? Then, when there was no doubt it was him
I thought, he's not here because of me. He's got work in Silverdale.
10 When he sees me he'll drop his eyes and walk on by like he never
saw me before, 'cause that's what Chippies do.

There were a lot more thoughts I've forgotten. It was my mind
trying to shield me, I guess – to protect me from disappointment by
refusing to believe or even to hope. If I'd let myself think he was
15 looking for me and it turned out he wasn't I couldn't have stood it.
I'd have fallen apart.

Anyway, the second passed and he saw me and I knew the miracle
had happened. He was here for me, all right – I could see it in his
face. He stopped, and I knew exactly how he was feeling – weak
20 knees, aching chest and a mind racing towards burnout.

It was just like an old, old movie. We stood looking at each other
and then we both moved at once, and before we knew it we were
clinging together in the middle of all that squalor and nothing
mattered except to hold on and never, ever, ever let go.

---

4 **go into overdrive**: start being very active   13 **shield** (v): protect   **disappointment**: sadness because sth. has not happened   17 **miracle**: wonder   20 **burnout**:
state of being extremely tired   23 **squalor**: dirty and unpleasant conditions

# DAZ

**26**   Its like she sez. i seen her and dam near got a hartatak. We run togevver and clingon and i forget abowt danger and all that.

So we clingon and i sez wot thay call you. Zoe she sez. i never herd ov it. i tel my name Daz and she larfs. wots funny i sez and she sez Daz thats a washing powda. wel i sez. Zoe sownd like a littel 5 animal or somfing and we boaf larfing.

lots more tork we done that firs nite. Magic it was only no magic in my riting so i stop now. you reed wot Zoe put, you be ther.

# ZOE

Yes, that's right – shove it all onto me, Daz. Typical flaming Chippy,
as Dad would say.

Ah, but he's right. It was magic. It was. I know it sounds corny
and all that, but you really do get so wrapped up in each other you
5 forget everything else. I mean, the guy was risking his life just being
there and we didn't even think about it. We were within a few yards
of the perimeter fence, a double fence with a floodlit walkway
between. All suburbs have them, and every now and then security
men patrol the walkway. They operate in pairs, some with dogs.
10 They all carry automatic weapons and a Chippy seen anywhere near
a fence after sundown is liable to get shot. There'd be TV cameras
dotted about as well, and guys in a post somewhere watching
screens. The lights had just come on and there'd be a patrol any
minute and there we were, him with this big yellow disc on his
15 overall and a Subby girl in his arms, horsing around and laughing as
if it were the most natural thing in the world. It's a wonder either of
us lived to tell the tale.

When we finally came up for air, Daz steered me toward a drift of
rubble which would hide us from the fence. The floodlights created
20 a pool of deep shadow on our side of the drift so that we'd be
practically invisible if anybody came along, which was unlikely. We
found a couple of big stones and sat down on them, holding hands.

There was so much to learn. So many things we didn't know
about each other. He began telling me how awful it had been,
25 thinking about me day and night, not knowing whether I was
thinking of him, and I said it'd been the same for me. He asked how

---

1 **flaming** (infml): used to emphasize that you are annoyed with sb./sth.  3 **corny**:
used too often to be interesting  7 **perimeter** [pə'rɪmɪtə]: outside edge of an area of
land  12 **dot sth.**: spread sth. over an area  15 **horse around** (infml): fool around
18 **steer**: move in a particular direction  19 **floodlight**: strong light used e.g.
outside of buildings  20 **drift**: large pile of sth. made by the wind

old I was and I told him I was nearly fifteen, though my birthday's in February and that was five months away. He said he'd just gone fifteen.

'D'you go to school?' I asked. I knew Chippies don't have to go, some do, some don't. He told me he got thrown out and when I asked why he grinned and said, 'Fooling around – thinking about you when I should've been thinking about my lessons.'

I nodded. 'I got in trouble for that too, but chucked out – that's a bit rough, surely?'

He shrugged. 'Big city. One school. Plenty kids waiting to go. I was gonna quit anyway.'

'What for? I mean, what d'you do now?'

'Nothing. I wanted to join Dred, only they turned me down.'

'You wanted –.' I looked at him. 'Why'd you want to be in a terrorist organisation, for Pete's sake?' I realised I knew pitifully little about him.

'Why?' He looked down, hacking the dirt with the heel of his trainer. 'They topped our Del for a kick-off. And I hate Subbies.'

'I'm a Subby.' Yes, I told myself. And here I am sitting in the dark with the guy. How do I know he's not fixing to cut my throat? I wasn't scared, though. I couldn't believe he'd hurt me. It was unthinkable.

'Yeah.' He loosened a small stone and flicked it away with his toe. 'I know. That's how come they knocked me back.'

'How d'you mean?'

'They saw us. You and me. At the club. They've got me figured for a Subby-lover.'

I nodded. 'My so-called friends've taken to calling me Chippy-lover.'

'Why?' He gripped my hands so tight it hurt. 'Do they know about me?'

'No.' I tried to free my hands. He realised what he was doing and relaxed his grip, but he seemed about to jump up and run.

---

8 **chuck sb. out** (infml): force sb. to leave a place   18 **kick-off** (infml): start

'No, they don't know about you. How could they? I didn't know about you myself till tonight, did I? And if I had, d'you think I'd have told anyone? I'm not a fool, Daz.'

He chuckled, shaking his head. 'Okay, Zoe. I'm jumpy, right?
5  They find me here, I die. For a minute I thought –.'

'Listen.' I looked in his eyes. 'I think you better go soon, anyway.' He'd laughed, but his reaction had reminded me of the risk he was taking. I told him he'd better go but I didn't want him to, and so to keep him I said, 'Who was Del?'

10  'My brother. He was fifteen.'

'And they – executed him?'

'Topped him, yeah.'

'What for.'

'Dred. Here in Silverdale two years back. I said I'd get even.'

15  'And will you?' I didn't want to know the answer to that. I don't know why I asked. He shrugged.

'Dunno. Spect so. Have to wait and see, won't we?'

He got up, so I did too. Muted voices and the clop of boots on cement told us a patrol was passing and we stood quietly till the
20  sound receded.

'Listen,' I murmured. 'You better not come here again, Daz. It's too dangerous, but how am I going to see you?'

He shook his head. 'I dunno, Zoe. There's only the tunnel. I gotta see you.'

25  'Maybe I could come to you.'

'D'you drive?'

'No. You've got to be seventeen.'

'How, then?'

'I don't know. Listen. Is there some way I can get a message to
30  you?' Mail service is confined to the suburbs and so is the phone, so I wasn't going to be able to write or call.

He thought for a minute, then said, 'Mebbe.'

---

4 **chuckle** (v): laugh quietly    14 **get even with sb.** (infml): cause sb. the same amount of trouble or harm as they have caused you    **spect** = expect    18 **muted**: quiet, not as loud as usual    20 **recede**: move gradually away

'How?'

'You know the guys who take your trash?'

'Yes I do, but – hey – you mean they'd take a note or something? Wouldn't they get in trouble?'

He laughed. 'Who's going to find one little bit of paper on a trash    5
truck? You slip 'em a little cash, they take your note. Tell 'em Daz at the Black Diamond. It's a club.'

It was obvious when you thought about it, but to me right then it was a wonderful discovery. A lifeline. A means of communication where I'd thought there could be none. For one thing, it meant we    10
could part tonight without too much anguish. It still wouldn't be perfect but it would be bearable.

And that's it. The story of our first date. I told him I'd think of a plan and write him, and meanwhile he was to look at the moon each night at ten and I'd be looking at it, too.    15

Romantic, right? And easy, because everything was going to be so much better now. So much better. Except that after he insisted on seeing me safely on to a well-lighted road, and kissed me, and melted away in the shadows, my blissful sleepwalk home was shattered first by a shout somewhere behind, then by that unmistakeable ripping    20
noise an auto rifle makes.

I tried to tell myself it had nothing to do with Daz but I knew better, and so after that one brief, ecstatic interlude it was back to square one, only worse.

---

8 **obvious** ['ɒbviəs]: clear    11 **anguish** ['æŋgwiʃ]: pain or unhappiness
12 **bearable** ['beərəbl]: *erträglich*    17 **insist on sth.**: demand that sth. happens
19 **blissful**: extremely happy    21 **auto rifle**: machine gun    23 **interlude**: period
of time between two events    23–24 **back to square one**: a return to the situation
you were in at the beginning of sth.

# DAZ

i kist her and it made me feel so grate i forgot wear i was. Not 4 long █28█
thogh. I'm walking under trees, finking i'm okay in the dark and all,
wen sudenly this dazzler hits me in the face and a voice sez hold it
rite ther.

5   i'm blind but not darft. i hang abowt, this guy eever gonna shoot
me or ast 4 my seeit witch i haven't got 1. Eever way it com 2 the
same fing so i run, nor i dont know wear i run neever.

He dont mess about. i'm dodging frou the trees and he showt
somfing and start shooting. bullits ratling twigs. i'm so scairt i cant
10  fink. i run and tork like this – wear the tunnel o god wears that
godam tunnel. i'm crying if you wanta know. Sum basted shoot at
you, you cry 2.

if this guy coud shoot i'm ded rite now. if he foller me, same. He
cant shoot and he dont foller, but wen the shooting stopt i know he
15  be calling his mates on radio. soon be milyons of em lucking 4 me. i
run til i seen the fence then cut left along it, blowing and torking
that tunnel o god wears it gon. Soon i'm in piles of muck and trash
and i fink this is it – that tunnel come owt somwear hear. jus then i
hear a big noyz and its a fan coming innit. Fans got spotlites plus
20  masheenguns. jus wot i need i dont fink. Fan coming in low over the
fence and i seen it spotlite racing over the grownd and i fink this is it
lad – you ded now 4 shor, but just then i seen the tunnel. i'm ded
nackerd but i run 2 it and get in nor i dont give a monkeys about no
miner tour neever.

25  Not much more 2 tel. i dont stop 2 swop doodies. i grab the bag
and set of, wynding in the twine. Slow job that wynding, speshly if
sum 1 after you wiv a gun. i dont yuse the flashlite 4 a bit in case
they seeit plus i cant stop 2 get it owt.

---

5 **darft** = daft: stupid in a silly way    8 **dodge** (v): move quickly and suddenly
to avoid sb.    9 **rattle sth.**: make a series of short loud sounds when hitting against
sth.    **twig**: *kleiner Zweig*    23 **nackerd** = knackered (BE sl): extremely tired
25 **swop sth.** (also: swap): give sth. to sb. and get sth. in exchange    26 **wind**
(**wound, wound**) **sth.** (in/up) [waɪnd]: *etwas aufrollen*

Aniway, no 1 after me. big noyz outside – yells, fans, shooting.
i dunno wot they shooting. each ovver i hoap. after i bang my hed
abowt six milyon times i stop and get my flashlite owt the bag and
evryfing fine after that. No miner tour. no Clint goast. Skelington stil
ther but so wot – damsite wors if he walking abowt rite?                    5

So i get hoam okay and that wen i start 2 worry. Zoe. she herd
shooting mebbe she fink i'm ded nor i cant tel her i'm not. Mebbe
they pick her up 4 Chippy-lover 2.

So big worry but worf it thogh. O yes.

Zoe.                                                                        10

---

5 **damsite** = damn sight (infml): very much

# ZOE

When I got home Mum wanted to know why there was mud on my shoes. It wasn't the number one topic on my mind. I told her I crossed the school playing-field. She didn't know anything about the name-calling and I wasn't about to tell her.

5  I couldn't eat. I mumbled some excuse about a big school lunch and cleaned up my shoes while my parents ate. After that I went to my room and tried to do my homework. I couldn't concentrate. A voice in my head kept saying, he could be dead. You were with him an hour ago and now he could be dead.

10  I'd have to watch the news. There's this bulletin at nine o'clock. Normally I'd have been walking back from youth club with Tabby at that time, but I couldn't go now. I told Mum I wasn't feeling too good and stayed in my room, looking out the window. If there weren't houses between I could've seen the fence from here, close to where

15  the tunnel was. As it was I could only see the faint radiance floodlights make in the sky.

Around seven the phone rang in the downstairs hallway. I hoped it was Tabby. Mum would say I was sick but at least it'd mean she was still allowed to associate with me.

20  It seemed like years till nine o'clock. At five to I switched on my set and caught the weather forecast. Wind and rain. Who cares?

There was nothing on the news. There wouldn't be in the main bulletin, of course, but there was nothing in the Silverdale spot, either. No news is good news, right?

25  Wrong. Not for me, anyway. I knew I was in for a sleepless night with plenty of tenterhooks before the next bulletin at six a.m.

I was right. If you've ever stayed awake all night – one of those long autumn nights – you'll know how the time can drag. I rolled around till my blankets got all knotted up. I drank water and looked

10 **bulletin** ['bʊlətɪn]: short news report on the radio or television    15 **radiance**: light shining from sth.    19 **associate with sb.**: spend time with sb.    26 **tenterhook**: cf. saying 'on tenterhooks': very anxious or excited while you are waiting to find out sth.

at my watch and went to the bathroom about eight hundred times and grew steadily more convinced that Daz was dead. Just before six I switched on with the volume real low and sat on the edge of my wrecked bed squinting at the screen and there is was, first item in the local news:                                                                                                   5

'There was an incident in south Silverdale last night when remote surveillance showed a man acting suspiciously near the perimeter fence. When challenged by a security guard the man, who was wearing outsider coveralls, fled, ignoring repeated orders to halt. The guard opened fire but the man made off into the darkness. An   10 exhaustive search failed to find him, and people living in the area are warned to be vigilant since the man is almost certainly dangerous and may be armed.'

Alive! My eyes burned, I looked like a lunatic in an old horror movie and I was starting a headache but I got up and danced round the   15 room, waving my arms, swooping by the mirror to grin at the frightful image I saw there. I took care not to stomp, because I didn't want to wake my parents. I realised I was probably the only person in Silverdale who was glad the intruder hadn't been shot, and I didn't care. Let them stare. Let them call me names. Let them ostracize me   20 for his sake if it suits their tiny minds.

He's alive.

---

4 **wrecked**: (hier) zerwühlt   **squint** (v): blinzeln   6–7 **remote surveillance**: Überwachung(sgerät)   11 **exhaustive**: including everything possible   12 **vigilant** ['vɪdʒɪlənt]: watchful   14 **lunatic** (n) ['luːnətɪk]: person who does crazy things 16 **swoop by sth.**: quickly move past sth.   17 **stomp**: walk with heavy steps 19 **intruder**: person who is somewhere where they are not wanted   20 **ostracize sb.**: refuse to let sb. be a member of a social group   21 **tiny**: very small

# DAZ

So Zoe knew i was okay but i dint know that. i'm worrid she be worrid so wot i done is, i went up 2 the dump. Dump is wear trash trucks go 2 empty plus the deepo is ther. i fort mebbe i fynd the crew wot graft rownd Zoe way and thay can slip her a noat. i know
5 wot Zoe way called. she told me.

i go up ther and ast arownd a bit and shorenuf i fynd the rite crew. 2 snags. 1 this fursday and thay dont work Zoe way til saterday. 2 crewboss nosy. 'What you,' he sez. 'Subby-lover or somfing?'

'Non ov yor biznis,' i sez.
10 'Not easy,' he sez, 'tork 2 a Subby kid. Trashman tork 2 Subby kids loos seeit, mebbe, loos job.' Corshous littel basted this crewboss but fond ov peanuts, same evrybody.

'Lissen' i sez. 'This Subby kid rich, rite? mebbe got peanuts 4 you, plus a noat 4 me. she be lucking owt 4 you, see – you chicken or
15 wot?'

He tuck my noat. 'fanks mate,' I sez. 'fanks a lot.' not easy 2 smuggel anifing in 2 Silverdale (or any ovver veezaville i gess) evry crew searcht at the gate. easy 2 smuggel stuff owt cos whos gonna fynd 1 littel fing in a truckful ov trash? aniway he tuck it and i'm
20 finking thats better. Zoe know i'm alrite saterday.

i'm going back frou the dump wen i herd futsteps behynd and sum 1 grab me and its Mick and a guy i dont know. thay frow me down in the muck and this guy neal on my back and twist my arm wile Mick jerk my hed up by the hare. 'Lissen,' he sez. 'This from
25 Cal. Cal knows you went frou the tunnel, got shot at. he finks mebbe the Subbies fynd the tunnel cos ov you.' he slam my face in the muck, jerk it up again. blud in my nose and mouf plus loos teef and eyes water. 'Cal sez stay owt ov that tunnel, understand?' i understand but befor i can tel him he slam me down again, jerk me up.
30 'Understand?' a gud explainer old Mick but i cant tork, mouf ful ov

3 **deepo** = depot ['di:poʊ]   6 **shorenuf** = sure enough

muck and blud and teef. i nod my hed a littel but he done it again aniway and i fink, hes gonna kill me, but he dont do it nomore. the ovver guy get of my back so i can breev, only not 2 gud breeving blud and snot and bits ov toof. i roll over and sit up, holding my face. Mick kick me in the kidnies, sez 'thay find that tunnel, we be 5 back 2 finish you.'

i sit a longtime holding my face witch it hurt very bad. no 1 com 2 help. You help Cal enemy, you Cal enemy 2 and no 1 needs that. So. i sit a longtime in the muck, then i get up and go hoam and tel our mam i fel off a nellifant. 10

'You darft our Daz,' she sez, and shes rite. And you know wot make me darft?

luv.

5 **kidnies** = kidneys: *Nieren*    10 **a nellifant** = an elephant

# ZOE

Saturday. One of those raw, foggy days when it never seems to get light. I'd written a note the night before and now I was hanging around with the thing in my pocket, waiting for the trash truck. I stood in the window looking down the garden. Naked trees, the
5 lawn and pathway slimy with fallen leaves. I hoped the truck would be early. I go for Tabby around ten on Saturdays and my parents might notice if I broke my routine.

Tabby had been sort of distant with me since my clash with Moncrieff over those stupid lines, though she had come up to me in
10 the schoolyard Thursday morning and said she hoped I was feeling better. I'd forgotten I was supposed to be sick and almost gave myself away. I told her it wasn't anything much and we chatted awhile, but there was a coolness about her which made me feel uncomfortable. It was as if in talking to me she was doing something she'd been
15 advised not to do, and I wouldn't be surprised at that.

It must've been my lucky day because the truck came quite early, and as it drew up Mum called me. I went through to the kitchen and she handed me a bag of trash. 'Be an angel and go put this by the can. It's almost full and they might as well take it.'
20 I could've hugged her. I'd dreamed up an excuse to go down the garden just as the crew arrived, but it wasn't nearly as good as this one. I grinned. 'Sure, Mum. It'll be a pleasure.' She probably thought I was nuts.

I took my time, and the garden gate opened just as I reached the
25 can. The crewman gave me a little nod, with his eyes down the way they do, but as I put down the sack he moved up real close, hissed, 'Here – take it,' and thrust a crumpled bit of paper in my hand.

I knew what it was and my heart kicked. I shoved it in my pocket, hoping nobody was watching from the house. As the guy went to
30 pick up the sack I drew out my own note and slipped it to him.

11–12 **give sb./sth. away**: jdn./etwas verraten   15 **advise sb. to do sth.**: tell sb. what you think they should do   20 **hug sb.**: put your arms around sb.   23 **be nuts**: be crazy

'Daz,' I whispered. 'Black Diamond. The money's for you.' I'd folded a couple of bills in the note. He nodded, looking past me at the house. I turned and walked away.

'Did that man speak to you?' asked Mum as I came in. She'd watched through the kitchen window. I nodded, trying to look cool. 5 'Yeah, y'know – rough weather, cold work. Something like that.'

'Well, I hope you didn't encourage him, dear. They're here to work, not fraternize.'

'I know, Mum. I didn't encourage him.' It must be tough having a Chippy-lover for a kid. 10

Like I said, it must've been my lucky day. The spelling wasn't hot but what he'd written was beautiful. I read it over till I had it by heart, then shredded the note and flushed it down the john. I hated doing that, but to keep it would've been just too dangerous. And after that I got my coat and set off for the Wentworth residence. My 15 luck might continue – who knows?

\* \* \*

It did continue, but it threw up a bit of a mystery as well. See what you make of it.

I arrived at five to ten and rang the bell. This Chippy girl, Zena, usually answers. She's a sort of maid but she doesn't live in. That's 20 not permitted, and I sometimes used to wonder how she coped with the contrast between the beautiful house she worked in all day and the dump she went back to at night. Anyway, she didn't answer this time. Nobody did at first, and I was just telling myself they weren't going to when an eye appeared at the peephole and the door opened, 25 and it was the guy himself. Paul Wentworth, Tabby's old man. He'd a peculiar look on his face and I thought, this is it – he's going to tell me to get lost, but he didn't. He said, 'Come on in, Zoe,' and as he said it his eyes were darting around like he was trying to see in all directions at once. He shut the door so fast I almost lost a foot. 30

11 **not (so/too) hot**: not very good in quality   13 **john** (infml): toilet   27 **peculiar** [pɪˈkjuːlɪə]: strange   28 **get lost** (infml): very unfriendly way of telling sb. to go away   29 **dart** (v): move suddenly and quickly

He took my coat and asked how I was and if Mum and Dad were well, but I could tell he was thinking about something else. He put me in the library (no, I'm not kidding – the Wentworth residence has its own library) and went off to get Tabby.

5　I was standing on a rug so thick it practically reached my knees, warming myself by the fire and gazing round at all the books when Tabby came in.

'Hi.' She grinned her old grin and I felt really good.

'Hi, Tabby,' I said. 'Where's Zena?'

10　'Oh, we – she's not here anymore. What shall we do today?'

Quick change of subject. I looked at her. 'Is something wrong, Tabby?'

She shook her head. 'No, 'course not. Why should there be?'

'Your Dad. He seemed – I dunno – sort of nervous. Has something 15 happened?'

'No. Not really. Listen.' She put her hand on my arm. 'If I'm a bit cool at school – if I seem to go along with the other kids when they tease you, it's because I have to, Zoe. I can't explain. Not now. But I want you to know I'm the same friend I always was.' She smiled 20 and squeezed my arm. 'We all are, in this house. Okay?'

I nodded and smiled and said okay, but I wasn't satisfied. I felt sure there was something going on that I wasn't supposed to ask about so I didn't, and we went up to Tabby's room and played some of her fabulous records and talked about boys and clothes and all 25 that, and lunchtime we went down Chiefy's for hamburgers, but it wasn't like it used to be. I'd intended telling her all about Daz – the notes and everything, but I didn't. At three-thirty when I was leaving she squeezed my arm again and said 'remember' with tears in her eyes, and I walked home not knowing whether the day had made 30 things better or worse.

And when I walked in the house the police were waiting.

\* \* \*

18 **tease sb.**: make fun of sb.　20 **squeeze**: press with your fingers

'Hello, Zoe. I'm Lieutenant Pohlman, Domestic Security. This is Sergeant Daws. We'd like to talk to you if that's all right.'

Domestic Security. Sounds cosy, right? Forget it. Domestic Security's the outfit that spies on Subbies and shoots Chippies. The outfit responsible for keeping us in and them out. They're the guys the government pays to keep everything jogging along exactly the way it is, and they'll do just about anything to see that it does. So when the lieutenant said we'd like, and if that's alright, I knew he wasn't offering me choices.

I don't mind admitting I was scared. Everybody's scared of DS, but I wasn't so much scared for myself as for Daz. Oh, I knew this could only be about him, and if DS knew about us then whatever they did to me would be nothing compared with what they'd do to him. I assumed they'd intercepted my note and I wondered briefly what had become of the trash crew.

Dad and Mum tried to talk to me but Pohlman got between us and said something to Daws and the sergeant ushered them out the room like it was his house and they were the callers. I heard Mum say she's fourteen for God's sake, and then the door closed and it was just me and the lieutenant.

He told me to sit down which was just as well, because I'd probably have fallen down if he hadn't. He took the other chair and said 'Where you been today, Zoe?' He was smiling and all like somebody's favourite uncle but he didn't fool me. I guessed my parents would have told him I was at Tabby's, so I told him that too.

'Tabby. That'd be Tabitha Wentworth, Paul Wentworth's kid, right?'

'Right.'

'They still let her see you?'

'I – sure they do. Why not?'

'You had some trouble in school, didn't you?'

'What trouble – what d'you mean?'

---

4 **outfit** (infml): group of people working together   **spy on sb.**: watch sb. secretly
14 **intercept sth.**: stop sth. that is going from one place to another from arriving
17 **usher sb. in/out**: show sb. where they should go   18 **caller**: visitor

'I think you know what I'm talking about, Zoe. I'm talking about Miss Moncrieff. About an imposition you did for her. I'm talking about brainwashing, Zoe.'

'Oh, that. Yeah, there was a bit of hassle about that. It's over now.'

5 'Is it?' he leaned forward, and he must be one of those guys who can't lean and smile at the same time because the smile faded.

'Is it over, Zoe? Don't some of the kids call you names? One name in particular? Don't they call you Chippy-lover?' His face got red as he spoke, and spit flew from his lips when he said Chippy. I

10 shrugged. 'Sure. Some do. I take no notice.'

This seemed to make him sore. 'You take no notice? Your friends call you Chippy-lover and you take no notice? Don't you like to have friends, or what?' He was almost shouting.

'They're not my friends.' I spoke softly. He sat back and ran his

15 tongue along his lip. 'Who are your friends, Zoe?'

'I dunno. I guess I don't have too many friends right now. Maybe I don't have any at all.' I wasn't about to give him names. The friend of a Chippy-lover is a Chippy-lover.

'Aw, come on.' The smile was back. 'It's not that bad, surely? You

20 have at least one friend, dontcha?'

'Do I?'

'Why, sure you do. Tabby. She's your friend, right? You just spent the day with her.'

'We – talked. It's not like it was.'

25 'Ah.' His eyebrows went up. 'Are you surprised about that, Zoe?'

'How d'you mean?'

'Does it surprise you that friends might want to withdraw their friendship from a person who makes trouble in the community?'

'I don't make trouble.'

30 He nodded. 'Oh, yes you do, Zoe. When you wrote brainwashing on that imposition, you were suggesting that the State tells lies to the people.' He smiled, but his eyes didn't. 'Now you may be too young

---

2 **imposition**: an unfair or unreasonable thing that sb. expects or asks you to do
6 **fade**: become less bright   9 **spit** (n): the liquid in your mouth   11 **sore** (adj):
angry   27 **withdraw sth.**: stop giving or offering sth. to sb.

to realise this, but when somebody communicates an idea like that
to others, it can do a lot of damage. People – some people – are liable
to start picking at bulletins, looking for inaccuracies. And of course
if you're looking too hard for something, you're liable to think you
found it even if it's not there.'                                                        5

I didn't say anything in answer to this. There was something
wrong with it, but I couldn't put my finger on it, and anyway I was
too nervous to argue with the lieutenant. They can put you in jail or
take away your citizenship. If you lose your citizenship you have to
leave your suburb and go live outside. You have no papers and no        10
rights. Bang – you're a Chippy.

By this time I was getting really confused. Why was Pohlman
interested in all this stuff about school? If they knew about Daz, why
didn't he say so and get it over? Maybe he was enjoying himself,
keeping me dangling. Or maybe –. I decided to find out once and for     15
all. I looked at him.

'Lieutenant Pohlman, have I done something illegal?'

He smiled thinly. 'I don't know, Zoe. Have you?'

This threw me. I mean, you don't expect DS to admit it doesn't
know. DS knows everything about everybody. It's the image. And it       20
seemed this wasn't about Daz after all. I guess I sort of gulped with a
mixture of surprise and relief, though I tried not to let the relief
show.

'No,' I said. 'I haven't, so why am I being questioned?'

'You're not being questioned, Zoe.' He chuckled.                        25

'You'd know it if you were. No – this is more in the way of a
warning. A shot across your bow if you like. It's our way of saying
we've got our eye on you, Zoe. You, and people like you. See, the
trouble with your sort is, you don't know when you're well off.
I mean, look around.' He made an expansive gesture. 'Silverdale,        30
right? Silverdale's got everything. Space, beauty, climate, all the

---

2–3 **liable to do sth.** ['laɪəbl]: likely to do sth.    3 **inaccuracy** (fml): mistake
19 **throw sb.** (infml): make sb. feel confused or surprised    21 **gulp**: *schlucken*
22 **relief**: feeling of happiness when sth. unpleasant stops    27 **a shot across the/**
**sb.'s bows**: sth. that you say or do as a warning to sb.    29 **well off**: rich
30 **expansive**: *ausladend*

amenities. You got theatres, clubs, bars, stadia, pools, restaurants –
every damn thing you can think of. You got nice houses and good
roads and schools and colleges and a university. And you've got the
most important thing of all, which is security. You're safe in
5   Silverdale, Zoe. Safe and snug. Nothing can touch you. Nothing can
hurt you. There are no hassles here. No problems.' He looked at me.
'Would you want to lose all that? Live outside? Is that what you
want?'

I shook my head and he said, 'Then why are you making waves,
10  kid? What do you want that you don't have already?'

I shrugged and smiled. 'I want it for everyone.'

'Hah!' He got up and bent over with his face about an inch away
from mine.

'Dreams, Zoe. Dangerous dreams. The world's the way it is, and
15  you better pray it stays this way because you're one of the lucky
ones.' He straightened and went to the door, pausing with his hand
on the handle to look back at me.

'You wouldn't last a week out there,' he said.

\* \* \*

The cops weren't out the door before my parents started in on me.
20  What did they want with you? What have you been doing, saying,
thinking? Is that it, or are they coming back? Do you have to report
anywhere, and if so when? Did you co-operate and were you polite?
I said, do we go straight into this second interrogation or do I get a
cup of coffee in between?

25   I got the coffee, and then I told them everything Pohlman said.
I was still feeling relieved they weren't on to Daz, but of course Mum
and Dad didn't know anything about that, and when I got through
Dad had a face on him like a man who's just been told he's gonna be
fed to crocodiles.

---

1 **amenity**: sth. that makes a place pleasant to live in

'That's it,' he said flatly. 'They'll be watching us from now on. All of us, because we're suspect.' He looked at me. 'I hope you're satisfied, young lady. I hope you know what it is you've done here.'

'What has she done, Gerald?' At least Mum was trying to stick up for me. 'She wrote some words, that's all. Some foolish words, and 5 the police have cautioned her. It's not the end of the world, for goodness' sake.' She looked at me. 'She'll behave in future and everything'll be just like it was.'

Dad shook his head. 'No, it won't. That's not the way it works, Amanda, and you know it.' He got up and went to the window and 10 stood with his hands in his pockets, looking out. 'Word gets around. Somebody says DS were at the Askew place last night, and somebody else says, Well, who'd have thought it – old Charlie. And before you know it they've got you figured for one of those FAIR guys or something and they stop putting business your way.' 15

'Fair guys?' I looked at Mum. 'What's a fair guy?'

Mum started to answer me but Dad broke in. 'FAIR. F.A.I.R. It stands for Fraternal Alliance for Integration through Reunification. It's a proscribed organisation, Zoe. An illegal, underground outfit whose members believe the world'd be a better place if we tore down 20 our fences and invited the Chippies to come share our lifestyle.' He laughed. 'They don't seem to realise our lifestyle would perish in about ten minutes after we did that, and most of us would perish with it. They're a bunch of spineless pinkos, and now folks're gonna think I'm one of 'em.' 25

'I'm sorry,' I said. 'I never even heard of FAIR. I didn't expect the cops to come running on account of a couple of words on a stupid imposition or I'd never have written them. And I can't believe such a small thing's going to affect you and Mum, anyway.'

He looked at me. 'You don't know, Zoe. You just don't understand. 30 Those people out there are full of hate. They want what we've got,

---

2 **suspect** (adj) ['--]: likely to commit a crime    4–5 **stick up for sb.**: support or defend sb.    6 **caution sb.**: warn sb.    11 **word gets around**: people talk 19 **proscribe sth.** (fml): say officially that sth. is not allowed    22 **perish**: be destroyed    24 **spineless**: weak and easily frightened    **pinko** (AE infml): a communist or a socialist

and these FAIR weirdos want to let 'em take it, even though it'll
destroy everything we've worked for. It's Pohlman's job to sniff out
those traitors, and I bet he thinks he's done just that.'

5 I didn't know what to say so I kept quiet, but I couldn't help
wondering what was so wonderful about a society where the cops
feel they have to watch what kids're writing, and a guy gets scared
for his reputation and his livelihood just because of something his
child did. Another thing I wondered was, what would Dad and
Mum and Pohlman think if they knew I meant to take the tunnel
10 into town tomorrow?

---

1 **weirdo** (infml): strange person   2 **sniff out sb./sth.** (infml): find sb./sth. by
looking   3 **traitor**: person who gives away secrets about their friends or country

# DAZ

32    She sends this crazy noat.

Half nine saterday nite i'm on my tod in the black diamond. Guy
shoves past, damnear nock me over. i rekernise the crewboss. he
don't say noffing but i find this paper in my pocket. i go in the bog
2 read it. shes only coming frou the tunnel tomorrow thats all.    5
i groan. Zoe i sez, you barmy. I cant go 2 that tunnel no more. i got
1 toof missing plus 2 black eyes plus soar all over. i go near that
tunnel 1 more tyme i'm ded.

i tear up the noat very littel. Frow it down the bog. i fink and fink
but its no yuse i gotta go. i'm more scairtn i bin in my hoal lyfe but    10
she be wayting down that tunnel 7 tomorrow nite so I gotta go.
Gudby world. so long our mam. sbin nise.

6 **barmy** (BE infml): slightly crazy

# ZOE

I had spare batteries in case my torch gave out, and two enormous     `33`
balls of knitting wool which I put in a plastic bag along with some of
my cassettes. The story was that Tabby invited me over when I was
there yesterday, but it nearly didn't work.

5    The visit from DS had really shaken my parents up. Mum had
even peeped into my room around three that morning to check
I hadn't slipped off somewhere, and all through Sunday if they
couldn't see me they kept calling to ask what I was doing.

I got worried. Suppose they wouldn't let me out of the house. It
10   seemed a distinct possibility. Daz would wait in the tunnel and I'd
never show up, and he wouldn't know why. He'd think I got caught
or lost underground or was lying in the dark with a broken leg or
something. He might try to find me, and he wouldn't have the twine
to guide him back.

15   The later it got the more nervous I felt. Daz had estimated the
tunnel at around three miles long, and I'd planned on giving myself
two hours to get through. I was meeting him at seven, so that meant
I had to leave home around four-thirty. This was unusually early to
be setting off for an evening with Tabby, and as the time drew near
20   I wished I'd planned it differently.

Anyway, four twenty-five rolled around and my bag was packed
and I couldn't stall any longer. 'Mum,' I called, coming downstairs.
'I'm going over to Tabby's to listen to music. I won't be late.' Mum
was in the kitchen. I was halfway to the door when she yelled 'Hey –
25   just a minute, young woman!' and appeared behind me with flour
on her hands. Two seconds later Dad came out the den. I stood
dangling my bag, looking from one to another.

'You're not going anyplace young lady,' said Dad. 'Not tonight.'

'Aw, but Dad – I promised.'

---

10 **distinct**: definite    15 **estimate sth.** (at sth.) ['estɪmeɪt]: guess    22 **stall** (v):
*etwas hinauszögern*    25 **flour**: white powder you need to make bread and biscuits
26 **den** (infml): room in a house where a person can work    27 **dangle**: swing freely

'Doesn't matter. You call Tabitha and tell her you won't be over after all 'cause your dad won't let you.'

'I can't tell Tabby that.'

'Well, you think of something then, because you're staying home and that's final.'                                                                              5

'Mum.' I turned to her, desperate, as you can imagine. 'Can't I just –.'

'You can just do as your father tells you, Zoe.'

This was it then. Disaster. I schlepped across to the phone with my heart in my socks. They stood watching me. I punched the      10
Wentworth code and stood with the receiver in one hand and my bag in the other. I daren't let go that bag.

There were a couple of clicks, and then a high-pitched screech that damn near blew my head off. I jerked the receiver away from my ear.                                                                            15

'What's wrong?' This from Dad.

'Dunno. Funny noise.' He came over and took it and put it to his ear. 'Hmm. Fault on the line, maybe.' He re-dialled and got the same result. I clutched at this straw.

'Mum – I can't just not show up. Tabby's my best friend. I don't      20
know what I'd do if she fell out with me.' My voice had a catch in it which wasn't entirely bogus.

Dad tried one more time and hung up. Mum said, 'She's right, Gerald – she can't just not show up.'

He looked at her, then at me. He shrugged. 'Okay, okay.' He      25
looked at his watch. 'It's four-thirty, Zoe. I want you back in this house at nine o'clock sharp. Sharp, d'you hear?'

'Yessir.' Never happen, I told myself, but it felt so good being off the hook I'd have promised anything.

* * *

6 **desperate**: *verzweifelt*   9 **schlep** (infml): go somewhere unwillingly   13 **high-pitched** (of sounds): very high   19 **clutch at a straw**: *sich an einen Strohhalm klammern*   21 **fall out with sb.**: have an argument with sb.   **catch** (n): sad tone   22 **bogus**: false   28–29 **be off the hook**: be free

It was scary in that tunnel even if you don't believe in ghosts and monsters and skeletons that walk, but the worst part was getting to the tunnel in the first place. It wasn't even properly dark yet, and I crept along expecting to be challenged any minute. DS could have
5 the area staked out after Daz's narrow escape, and they might be watching me, anyway. Maybe they'd installed extra cameras or found the tunnel and sealed it. I didn't know what I'd say if some bouncer stopped me and searched my bag.

'Oh, I thought I'd just sit inside this old sewer pipe awhile and
10 knit some covers for my cassettes. Pretty colour, isn't it?'

Anyway, I didn't meet anybody and I set off through the tunnel, letting out my wool and trying to remember what Daz had told me about the trip. I reached the foot of the rusty ladder at six thirty-five. Either I'd made good time in the conditions or it wasn't three miles.

15 I leaned on the ladder to wait. I thought I'd be smart and save my batteries by switching off. If you're not moving you don't need to see, right? Well, no, but it's just amazing the noises you hear, the stuff you imagine when you're alone in the dark. I kept switching on and off, and in the end I gave up and left it on, jammed in a crack in
20 the wall. It was better, but it didn't keep me from wondering if this was the right ladder.

He showed up four minutes early and I hardly recognised him, his face was such a mess. He was moving slow and he flinched and gasped when I squeezed him.

25 'What the heck happened to you?' I asked.

He told me. When he was through I said 'I'm sorry. This whole thing is so dangerous for you. You shouldn't have come.'

He laughed. 'And what if I hadn't? What would you have done – waited here till you died or what? Anyway, you know I can't stay
30 away from you.'

It was good for a while after that. I forgot where we were, and the danger we were in. I forgot the time too, until we came out of a long

---

4 **challenge sb.**: order sb. to stop and say who they are   5 **stake sth. out**: watch a place secretly, esp. for signs of illegal activity   9 **sewer pipe**: *Abflussrohr*

clinch and he said, 'When d'you have to be home?' as though we were on a regular date or something. I held my wrist in the torchlight so I could see my watch. It was eight o'clock.

'I don't want to go back, Daz,' I said. 'I want to be with you all the time.'                                                                                    5

'I know.' He held me. 'I want that too, but it can't happen and that's a fact. They've got us penned up in separate cages and there's no way out. We can't even see each other this way anymore.'

I knew that. I'd been trying not to think about it. Now the realisation hit me like a truck. I broke away from him. 'It's not fair!'   10
I cried. Fair, fair, fair, went the echo. 'Why should we live behind wire like something in a zoo?'

'Hey – sssh!' Daz caught hold of me, covered my mouth with hard fingers. 'They'll hear us up there.'

'Okay.' I shook my head and he took his hand away. 'But it's not   15
right, Daz. It's not. People're just people, and when they love someone it's wrong to keep them apart.' I started to cry. I tried to stop myself but I couldn't. 'Who says, Daz? Who says we've got to live the way we do? Who are they, and what gives them the right?'

'Sssh.' He stroked my hair. For a husky guy he was surprisingly   20
gentle. 'They're the government, Zoe, that's who they are. Nothing gives 'em the right – nothing can – but you see they don't need the right 'cause they've got the power. They've got it forever, too, 'cause only their friends get to vote.' He laughed. 'What d'you think Dred's about? Why d'you think guys and women get theirselves kilt all the   25
time like that?'

I shook my head and he said, 'To break the power, Zoe. To get it away from them and give it to us.' I shook my head again.

'It doesn't work, Daz. All it does is cause more wire. More lights. More cops. There's got to be another way.'                                              30

'Yeah?' He looked down at me. 'What other way?'

'What about FAIR?' I murmured.

---

1 **clinch** (n) (infml): position in which two lovers hold each other tightly   7 **pen
sb. up**: shut an animal or a person in a small space   10 **realisation**: process of
becoming aware of sth.

'FAIR?' He laughed. 'That bunch of nerds? What d'you think they're gonna do, Zoe?'

'They want us all to live together, don't they?'

'Oh, sure. And what do they do about it? I'll tell you. They have
5  secret meetings. They print handbills and stick 'em on subway walls. Oh – and they like to be nice to Chippies, only not too nice or the lornorders might get suspicious.' He snorted. 'What good d'you think that'll do, Zoe?'

I shrugged. 'I dunno, Daz, but at least somebody's trying to do
10  something. I wish –.'

'What?'

'I wish something would happen right now, or real soon. I don't want to wind up like Grandma, grieving for some guy she last saw eighty-eight years ago.'

15  We kissed then, and clung to each other but time was against us and we knew we were only prolonging the agony. I'm not going to go on about it. If you love someone – really love them, and if you can imagine how it'd feel to leave them with a very strong chance you'd never meet again – ever – then you've got it. And if you don't,
20  and can't, it's no use my trying to put it into words.

I cried all the way back through the tunnel. All the way. Crying sounds real sad where there's echoing. It's the sound of total desolation. I didn't care much if I got out or lost myself down there in the dark, but I guess I must've followed the wool because after
25  what seemed a long time I felt moving air on my wet cheeks and there I was, back in the cage.

I walked in home around ten-fifteen and it must've been obvious to my parents I'd been weeping. I walked in expecting to catch hell, but I guess they thought something had happened between Tabby
30  and me, because they didn't say anything. When Mum asked was I all right and I burst into tears and ran up to my room, nobody followed.

---

5 **handbill**: small printed advertisement given to people by hand   13 **wind up** (infml): find yourself in an unexpected situation or place   16 **prolong sth.**: make sth. last longer   **agony**: extreme pain   23 **desolation**: feeling of being very lonely and unhappy   28 **catch hell** (infml): be punished or spoken to angrily about sth.

* * *

Monday morning. School. Those used to be my two least favourite things. Now that Pohlman's visit had screwed everything up at home I was glad it was Monday. Glad to be out the house and biking, wrapped in mist, the shiny wet roadway to school.

Not that school was a million laughs, mind. There was still the name-calling and the ostracizing and all that. Even the teachers seemed cool toward me, though that could be just psychological.

No. The reason I wanted to be in school was Tabby. When you've only one friend you worry about her. You need to know where she is and what she's doing and if she's still your friend. You get a bit obsessive, in fact. And that's how I was about Tabby. You might think all this stuff with Daz would sort of push her into the background, and maybe it would have if he could be with me. As it was, the miles and the wire between him and me made me need her even more. I was afraid of this need. Afraid I might cling and that this clinging would smother her, drive her away. I wished she needed me.

What I wanted to do was tell her about Daz. I don't know if you've ever had a secret. A really heavy one. If you have you'll know what a relief it is to tell someone. And that's what I was going to do that Monday morning.

Except she wasn't there.

I searched the yard and the locker room and there was no sign of her. She wasn't in Mr Pawley's at registration. Right after registration I went along to the office and asked the secretary if anybody had called to say Tabby was sick. Mrs Corrigan gave me the sort of look everybody seemed to be giving me these days and said nobody had.

I went to my physics class. I've never liked physics and I couldn't concentrate. I made a stupid mistake and Mr Collins humiliated me in front of the class. Some of the kids had guessed what was bugging

---

11 **obsessive**: thinking too much about sb./sth.   16 **smother**: kill sb. by covering their face so that they cannot breathe   23–24 **registration**: time when a teacher looks at the list of students and checks that the students are present

me and snickered, casting meaningful glances at Tabby's vacant seat. At breaktime I checked the office again, then went to the locker room.

Tabby's locker was next to mine. As I approached, I saw with
5 relief that its door was open. That meant she'd arrived and was somewhere around. I hurried forward.

The locker was empty. Somebody had cleaned it out and left the door wide open. They'd even torn down her Invaders picture. I checked around to make sure the thief hadn't just dumped everything
10 on the floor, then made my way back to the office and rapped on the glass.

Mrs Corrigan slid the panel aside. 'Yes?'

'Tabitha Wentworth's locker, Mrs Corrigan. Somebody broke into it and took all her stuff.'

15 The secretary pursed up her lips and looked at me as though I was some kind of retard. 'No, Zoe Askew, they have not. Lawson has removed Miss Wentworth's property because she won't be returning to school.'

'Won't be –?' Lawson's the janitor. He only empties your locker if
20 you died or something. 'Why?' I stared at her. My heart was kicking so hard my chest hurt. I gripped the counter. 'What's happened to Tabby, Mrs Corrigan? Where is she?'

'Don't shout, child.' She straightened some papers on her desk, not looking at me. 'I imagine your friend is at home, and if you take
25 my advice you'll stay away from her.'

'Why? Is she sick? Is she going to die?'

Mrs Corrigan secured the sheaf of papers with a clip. 'I can tell you nothing more, Zoe. Tabitha Wentworth has left this school and will not return. And now if you'll excuse me I have work to do.' She
30 reached out without looking at me and closed the panel.

The buzzer sounded end of break. I had an English class but I knew I was going to cut it. I had to. I'd die if I didn't find out what

---

1 **snicker**: laugh in a quiet, unpleasant way  **cast sth.** (v): look in a particular direction  **vacant**: empty  16 **retard** (n, sl) ['– –]: rude way of describing sb. who is not intelligent  19 **janitor**: man who looks after a building  21 **chest**: *Brustkorb*
27 **sheaf**: a number of pieces of paper

had happened to Tabby, and it was obvious nobody around here was going to tell me.

I sneaked off. That isn't hard to do when a school's got a thousand kids in it. I left my bike and just walked away across the playing field, keeping some outbuildings between me and the admin block,    5 and got through a hole in the fence. I followed the fence along till I hit the road and headed for Tabby's place.

* * *

I turned into Wentworth Drive and stopped dead. There was a cop at the bottom of Tabby's driveway. He was standing with his hands behind his back, looking across the street. My first thought was    10 murder. Not long ago in a place called Summerhill a whole family had been murdered by the maid and the gardener, but surely there'd be more than one cop if it was something like that. Whole place'd be crawling. There'd be cars and an ambulance and the usual crowd of media ghouls.    15

Not murder, then. Some sort of accident? No, for the same reasons. And I could see there hadn't been a fire.

The house nearest to me – the corner house – looked quiet. The door was shut, and so were all the windows I could see. The garage door stood open and it was empty. No vehicle was parked in the    20 driveway or at the curb. The cop was still looking in front of him. I set off up the driveway and was glad when I put the house between us.

I crossed the backyards. Five of them. I had to climb two fences, skirt three empty pools and crawl through a lot of wet bushes.    25 I scared a cat and heard a dog and saw a Chippy maid in the window of house number four. She didn't see me.

Tabby was on the backporch, sitting on the step. She stayed there when I walked out of the shrubbery, and that's when I knew it must be bad. I went over and she squinted up at me and I saw she'd been    30 crying.

---

15 **ghoul** [guːl]: person who is too interested in unpleasant things    25 **skirt sth.**: go around the edge of sth.

'What're you doing here, Zoe? Why aren't you in school?'

I looked at her. 'I don't – what's up, Tabby? What's happened? They said you left.'

She nodded glumly. 'I did.'

5 'But why? Are your folks moving or what? You never said anything and I thought we were friends.'

She shook her head. 'You don't need friends like me, Zoe. I'd fade if I were you, before somebody sees you here.'

'What're you talking about, Tabby?' I hunkered down and gripped
10 her shoulders. 'Why shouldn't I be here? Tell me.'

She shook her head, avoiding my eyes. Her mouth twisted up. 'We are moving Zoe, but not through choice. We have to go tomorrow because –.' Her control snapped. She howled and threw her arms round me. 'They've kicked us out, Zoe. We can't stay here
15 anymore.'

I held her while she wept, her face buried in my shoulder. I stroked her hair as things started coming together in my mind.

'Your parents?' I said softly, 'They're in FAIR, right?'

She moved her head in mute affirmation. I didn't know what to
20 say after that so I just held her. Little by little she grew quiet, and after a while she whispered, 'Go away, Zoe. There's a cop out front. If they find you here they'll think you're one of us.'

I hugged her. 'I am, Tabby. I know that now. I think I always was. That's been my trouble all along. What I can't understand is why
25 your dad – I mean he's rich, important, all that. Why'd he want to change things, Tab?'

She shrugged. 'I don't know, Zoe. Conscience? I mean, we all know what's right and what isn't, don't we? Even if we don't want to. I guess maybe he couldn't just sit back and enjoy all the good things
30 he had, knowing there are people out there starving. And he's right, Zoe. They can kick us out and do whatever they want to do, but it won't alter the fact that he's right and they're wrong.'

---

4 **glum**: sad, quiet    7 **fade** (infml): disappear    9 **hunker down**: sit on your
heels with your knees bent up in front of you    13 **snap**: break suddenly    **howl**:
make a loud cry when you are in pain or angry    19 **affirmation**: *Zustimmung*
27 **conscience**: *Gewissen*

'Listen!' I squeezed her and she lifted her head. 'I want to tell you something, Tabby.'

I told her everything. How Grandma'd always talked to me about the way it used to be. How I'd fallen for Daz that night at the Blue Moon. Our meetings and letters. Pohlman's visit. Everything. By the time I'd finished she'd dried her eyes and blown her nose and got herself pretty much together. She looked at me.

'I'm glad you told me, Zoe,' she said. 'I had no idea. But you certainly shouldn't be here when you know the police are watching you. They could decide to kick you and your parents out too, y'know.'

'I don't care, Tabby. I don't know if I want to go on living here anyway, now that you're going.'

She shook her head. 'Don't talk that way, Zoe. Silverdale's not so bad. You may be a little low on friends right now, but at least you get to eat every day and sleep in a warm bed nights.'

'Oh, Tabby – I'm sorry.' I'd been so wrapped up in my own little misfortunes I'd hardly spared a thought for the Wentworths' awful plight. I took her hand in mine. 'What'll you do, Tabby? Where will you go?'

'Oh.' She managed a watery smile. 'I didn't mean – it's not that bad, Zoe. Not for us. I mean, we won't starve or have to sleep in the woods or anything. We've got a place.'

I looked at her. 'What sort of place? Where?'

'A house. I don't know exactly where, but it's way out in the country. Dad started building it a long time ago, when he and Mum first got involved with FAIR.' She smiled again. 'Being rich and in real estate has its advantages. So you see – you won't have to imagine us cooking rats and possums over a woodfire and sleeping in the rain.'

---

17 **be wrapped up in sth.**: be so involved with sth. that you do not pay enough attention to other people or things   18 **misfortune**: bad luck   **spare a thought for sb.**: think about sb.   19 **plight**: difficult and sad situation   22 **starve**: die from hunger   29 **possum** = opossum

'No.' I wrapped my arms round my knees. 'I'm glad about that, Tabby. But I still don't understand how it's gonna work for you. I mean, money and all that. Your dad won't be in real estate anymore.'

She shrugged. 'I don't know about any of that either, but I bet 5 Dad's got it all figured. He's a real smart cookie, my dad.'

'I know.' I gazed down the backyard, wondering whose view this was going to be. 'I wish I was coming with you.'

'No, you don't. It sounds okay now, but I'm sure we'll have all kinds of problems out there. You stay and finish school and keep on 10 thinking the way you do and maybe things'll change.'

She smiled. 'Maybe you'll be the one to change 'em, then you and Daz'll be together. And in the meantime there's always Grandma.'

I shook my head. 'Not always, Tabby. She's a hundred and four, y'know.'

15 'Yeah, well –.'

We sat looking down the yard, not saying anything. After a while the door opened behind us and Mrs Wentworth came out. Her eyes were red. I thought she might make me go away but she didn't. She set milk and cookies on the top step and left us to say our goodbyes.

20 I went home. School wasn't out yet, but I went home anyway, and you know it's just amazing the things you can discover by arriving home unexpectedly in the middle of the afternoon.

\* \* \*

Mum looked up from her magazine. 'Zoe. What're you doing home? It's only two thirty.' There was something in her voice that might be 25 apprehension. I thought she was afraid I'd got myself into more trouble at school so I said, 'It's okay, Mum. It's not me this time, it's Tabby.' I thought she'd ask what about Tabby but she didn't. She said, 'It had to be today, didn't it? You never come home earlier than three-thirty and it had to be today.'

---

25 **apprehension**: worry or fear that sth. unpleasant may happen

She sounded weary, resigned. This wasn't like her and fear flickered in me, deep down. 'What does that mean, Mum? What's so special about today that I shouldn't –.'

I broke off, listening. Footfalls above my head. Voices. Dad's and another, upstairs. I remembered there'd been an unfamiliar car at the curb when I came by just now. I looked at her. 'Who's upstairs, Mum? What's going on here?'

'Now, Zoe.' She got up. The magazine slid off her lap and she stepped on it and sort of tottered toward me with her arms out. 'You're not to get upset.'

She tried to take me in her arms but I shook my head and turned away. 'No, Mum. Don't do that. You've done something, you and Dad. Don't baby me. Tell me what it is.'

She dropped her arms and sighed. 'We meant to break it to you gently, dear. We didn't want you to find out this way, but how were we to know you'd come home in the middle –.'

'Tell me!' It was a shout. A scream. I couldn't help it. My fists were clenched so tight they were trembling and I was showing my teeth. I must've looked like a wild animal and my mother recoiled with a small cry.

'Your father sold the house.'

Ah. I turned to the window, bracing my hands on the sill, resting my forehead on the cold pane which fogged with my breath. So that's it. I should've known. It's tainted for them now, this house. This formerly respectable house which is respectable no longer because the police were here. Because it could be under surveillance and people know. Ah, yes. That's the clincher. People know.

I closed my eyes. Behind me, Mum was silent. I heard Dad and the other guy come downstairs. The house door opened and they

1 **weary**: tired    4 **footfall**: sound of sb. walking    9 **totter**: walk or move with weak, unsteady steps    18 **clenched**: *geballt*    **tremble**: shake    19 **recoil**: move your body quickly away from sb. because you find them frightening or unpleasant    22 **(window)sill**: *Fensterbrett*    24 **taint sth.** (fml): damage the opinion that people have of sth.    26 **surveillance**: observation    27 **clincher** (infml): *entscheidendes Argument*

stood talking, keeping it low. I wondered what the guy'd made of my
outburst a moment ago. Not that I gave a damn.

It wasn't just the house we'd be leaving. I knew that before the
guy drove off and Dad came in and told me. Silverdale's not that big.
5 You can't hide in it. You can't run away from something by moving
house. What's known, if it's worth knowing, is known all over the
suburb. You move and it'll follow you. No. The only way to wipe the
slate clean and start over is to find another suburb. And that's what
Dad had done. It was called Peacehaven, it was more than a hundred
10 miles away and he'd bought a house there.

So. Goodbye Tabby, hometown, Grandma, Daz. Little Zoe's
leaving you 'cause Daddy knows best. Daddy can't wait to get his
little girl away to that nice, clean place where the past can't reach
and there are no bad influences. Daddy's really looking forward to it.
15   Don't hold your breath, Daddy.

---

7–8 **wipe the slate clean**: forget about past mistakes and start again
15 **don't hold your breath**: used to say that sth. will take long or may not happen

# DAZ

34 leaving Zoe maid me feal so bad i coud dye. it woz late wen i got hoam but no yuse trying 2 sleap. Our mam in bed, so i tuck some doody stamps and some tucker stamps and trade them 2 a guy i know 4 peanuts. the idea is get smasht rite?

i dont go in that Blue Moon a longtyme now. i fink mebbe peeple   5
remember how i get them Subbys away that tyme, plus Mick ther most nites. Mick see wot he done 2 my face he larf. tonite i dont care. its late and a long walk 2 that ovver club Black Diamond so i go in Blue Moon.

No trubble. Mebbe no 1 rekernise me wiv my mestup face but no   10
1 tork 2 me neever. i stand on my tod in a corna, nokking them back. this fing i'm drinking call a mixtup rite, cos 5 diffrent drinks init plus it gets you mixtup. Subbys call it lob otter miser. aniway i get 3 ov them mixtups down or 4 mebbe 5 and evryfing going rownd and rownd and i cant fink no more not even abowt Zoe and   15
some 1 near me torking. i rekernise the voyce. i get my eyes lyned up and start my brain and its this guy wot beet up on me wiv Mick. hes torking 2 anovver guy. my lughoals not heering 2 gud plus my brain keep stopping but i heer Wentworf. Zoe frend call Wentworf. i moov up close 2 earwig.   20

i heer this. Lornorders kick Wentworf famly outer Silverdale Toozday. rich famly, bring lotsa gud stuff owt wiv em. 1 man 1 wumin 1 kid. thay come owt, this guy wayting 4 them wiv his mates. kill the Subbys nik ther stuff.

i fink, this kid Zoe frend. i gotta do somfing. i finish my mixtup,   25
leeve. owtside i cant wolk 2 gud i hit 1 howse bounce of hit anovver howse fall down larfing, sleap.

---

3 **tucker** (infml): food    18 **lughole** (BE): ear    20 **earwig**: listen secretly to what other people are saying    24 **nick sth.** (infml): steal sth.

# ZOE

'Oh hello, Zoe. I've been expecting you.' Grandma moved aside so I could come in, and closed the door behind me. 'Go through. I'll get coffee.'

'I didn't come for coffee, Grandma.'

5  'I know, child, but a good cup of coffee never hurt, and waiting for it'll give you time to cool off. Sit down.'

I sat but I didn't cool off. The way I was feeling, that wouldn't have been possible. I gazed out the window, seeing nothing, picking at the knee of my jeans.

10  Grandma brought in the coffee, poured and sat down. 'They told you, then?'

'Only because they had to. I came home early, caught 'em selling the place. Otherwise they'd probably have told me on the way to the airport.'

15  'I don't think that's quite fair, dear.'

'Fair?' I looked at her. 'What's fair got to do with it, Grandma? D'you think it's fair to take someone away from everything they've ever known without even talking to them about it first?'

She shook her head. 'I don't, and I said so to your mum and dad, 20  but they thought they were handling it right.'

'Well, I'm not going, so there.'

'Now, don't be silly, dear. Your parents have decided to move, and since you are not yet old enough to look after yourself you have no choice but to go with them.'

25  'I could stay here with you.'

She shook her head. 'No, Zoe, you could not, for three reasons. One – your parents would never agree. Two – I have only the one little bedroom. And three – I'm a hundred and four years old and it takes me all my time to take care of myself.'

30  'I'd help you. I could clean the apartment and cook and all like that. I'm not a little kid.'

'Zoe.' She leaned forward and took my hands in hers. 'I know how you feel but it's no use – the decision's been made. I don't like it any more than you do but we're not in control, child.' She smiled and squeezed my hands. 'You'll make new friends, wait and see. Once you're there, it won't be nearly as bad as you think.'

'Oh, Grandma. You're just saying the sort of stuff all adults say to kids. I thought you were different. You always used to be.'

She smiled, but it was a sad smile. 'What did you want me to say, 5 Zoe? Run away? Leave Silverdale in the middle of the night, go be a Chippy? Is that what you expected?'

I nodded. 'That, or something like it, yes.' I looked into her eyes. 'Why shouldn't I run away, Grandma? I could go to Daz. He'd look after me.' 10

'Daz?'

'The guy I met. You know – the one I told you about?'

She nodded. 'He got in touch?'

'We've met up, Grandma. Twice. He's been here in Silverdale and I've been out.' 15

'Oh, Zoe!' She squeezed my hands so hard her rings dug in. 'That is so dangerous, dear. If DS knew you were fraternising with someone from outside they could make you leave Silverdale – your dad and mum too – and live as Chippies for the rest of your lives. Did you know that?' 20

I nodded. 'I know. The Wentworths leave tomorrow.'

'Paul Wentworth?'

'Yes. And his wife and my best friend Tabby. They're in FAIR.'

'How come you know about this, Zoe?'

'Tabby told me.' 25

'Ah. Huh. Well, that's a pity. Just when we –.' She let go my hand and sat back. 'I can see now why you're so upset, you poor thing. First your best friend, then your home, and all in a day, too. And Daz, of course.'

She didn't say anything after that. She folded her knotty, thin 30 hands in her lap and sat looking at them. I drank my coffee, watching her over the rim of the cup. Maybe I wouldn't have to move to Peacehaven after all.

30 **knotty**: *knotig*

It was nothing like that. Later, I was to find out she'd been brooding about something far more important than my problem, but at the time I thought she was thinking up a plan. You can imagine my disappointment when she looked at me and said, 'I wish
5  there was some way I could make all of this easier for you, Zoe, but there isn't.'

I went home and found my parents packing. Dad said 'We leave Friday.' I didn't say anything.

I had my thoughts, though.

2 **brood about sth.**: think a lot about sth.

# DAZ

**36** Monday i woak up erly. You sleap all cold nite on crack stoans you wake up erly 2. my hed banging plus i feal pukey but i remember I got somfing 2 do.

Firs gorra gerra gun.

Easy. Dred got moast of the guns but i know wear is 1. our Del    5
put 1 gun under the flor at hoam. after thay topt him sumtymes wen our mam owt i tuck it owt luck at it. fink, sumday i kill 1 Subby wiv this 4 our Del. This gun bilong 2 Dred but our Mam dont know its ther and I never turnd it in.

i ronik innit? me keeping this gun 2 kill 1 Subby now i'm gonna    10
yuse it 2 save 3.

Nex fing. wear this guy gonna hambush them Subbys? Not near Silverdale 4 shor. Start shooting near Silverdale, fans com shoot you. Moas kickout Subbys hed 4 town, luck 4 old howse 2 liv in. So. This hambush probly sumwear between Silverdale and town. gorra get    15
myself hid tonite, foller the guy. i hoap hes only got 4 mates – our Del gun got 5 bullits.

i cleenup, get my hed down 2 be fresh 4 the job. wear you going sez our mam wen i'm leeving arownd 9. No wear Mam i sez. No yuse her worrying. i can worry enuff 4 2.    20

---

2 **pukey** (infml): as if you had to throw up    4 **gorra gerra** = got to get a
12 **hambush** = ambush sb.: make a surprise attack on sb.

# ZOE

I didn't go to school Tuesday. My parents thought I did, but I didn't 37
see why I should expose myself to the sort of hassle I'd been getting
there, for the sake of three more days. And anyway I had some
thinking to do.

5    First I thought I'd go round to Tabby's, maybe see her one more
time, but I decided the Wentworths'd have enough to do without me
hanging around, plus I didn't know if I could stand another of those
goodbyes. So I went to the park and sat on a bench by the pond
where there are ducks but very few people this time of year.

10    I'd been awake most of the night trying to decide what to do. I'd
tried to image what it'd be like to be a hundred miles away from
Daz, knowing for certain we were never going to meet again and not
even able to communicate through notes. I couldn't do it. I thought
about Tabby, and I thought about Grandma. Mum had told me she

15   and Dad had offered to take Grandma to Peacehaven too but she
refused, saying she liked her own place, that her life was in Silverdale.
I've always loved Grandma, and the thought of being way up there
in Peacehaven without her to talk to was more than I could bear. So,
with dawn in my window I decided that whatever happened I would

20   not go to Peacehaven, and with that I fell asleep.

It's easy to make brave vows when you're tucked up snug in bed.
There, dream and reality get mixed up even if you're awake. In the
grey light of morning, huddled in my coat under that steely cold sky
it seemed a lot harder. I was still determined to do it, but now I was

25   having to face up to the difficulties, and there were many.

First, I had to get out of Silverdale. That may not sound so hard
but I don't drive, and they don't let you walk out. There was the
tunnel, of course, but I didn't dare contemplate using that when DS
might be watching. There'd be no point getting away and then being

30   killed by Dred for betraying their route into the suburb.

2 **expose oneself to sth.**: put oneself in an unpleasant situation   19 **dawn**:
daybreak   21 **vow**: formal and serious promise   28 **contemplate**: consider, think
about   30 **betray sth.**: give information to an enemy

Then if I did get out, how would I live? There was no work out there, and I was too young to qualify for the government food stamps and clothing vouchers most Chippies exist on. I'd be relying on Daz, but what if he couldn't help? I was beginning to realise I knew nothing about his circumstances, except he had a mother and 5 they lived in the highest apartment block in Rawhampton. Would Daz's mother be prepared to feed me? Would she be able to? And anyway, why should she?

And then there's Mum and Dad. Okay, so they haven't been all that supportive toward me lately, but they're my parents and I love 10 them. Once I go through that wire, I've lost them forever. With me outside, it won't matter whether they're here in Silverdale or a hundred miles away in Peacehaven, I'll never see them again. And that goes for Grandma too, of course. If I run away, I'll be leaving her far more finally than if I went with Mum and Dad. Flights and 15 freeways link all suburbs, no matter how remote, but nothing spans the yawning chasm that lies between Veezaville and Chippyland.

After a while I got chilled sitting on the bench and some little kids came to feed the ducks, so I got up and went off to try to find out where the trash trucks work on Wednesdays. 20

---

3–4 **rely on sb.**: need or depend on sb.    10 **supportive**: giving help    16 **remote**: far away    **span** (v): stretch from one side to the other    17 **yawning chasm** ['kæzəm] (fml): difference so big it is difficult to overcome

# DAZ

i hed norf. Owt past wear the tunnel is 2 wear the bildings fin owt  38
and all fall down. no 1 livs hear. 2 near Silverdale. 2 near lornorders
but gud place 4 hambush. Kickowt Subbys moasly come here firs,
spend the nite. i get down behynd a bit ov wall, Del gun handy, wait.
5    4 a longtyme noffing. i start finking mebbe i got the rong place
plus i'm ded cold then i heer som littel fing lyke some 1 kick a stoan.
i luck owt and i see 2 guys coming lyke mooving shadders, sept
shadders dont hav ryfels, rite? Thay creep rite by me. i luck 2 see
ovvers com but no 1 else. i'm glad thers oanly 2. Thay past me and
10  i foller littel bit norf littel bit norf til thay fynd a spot thay lyke. Thay
all the tyme torking so dont heer me. thay hyde in 2 ruins, 1 this
syde the street 1 the ovver but torking acrost lyke on a picnic or
somfing. i fink if Cal seen em he larf or mebbe shoot em in the mouf.
i get behynd the 1 wot don me over. i never fyred a gun but coudn
15  miss from hear.

we settel down, wait 4 morning. longtyme. i seen 1 rat and 1 fin
dog plus i heer a lot ov rabbit witch it coms from the guys moufs.

i'm frozen. glad wen i seen it start 2 com lite. gorra be careful now
thogh or som 1 spot me.

20  waiting waiting waiting. Sunup now but no warmf init. no
Subbys neever. i get in payshent, fink wy wait 4 Subbys? oanly 2 ov
em. shoot em now get it don wiv.

boaf guys worrid now torking acrost the street wear ar thay? wy
thay not com? lucking norf, never luck behynd. i pickup Del gun,
25  my fingers feal stiff wiv cowld plus i got the shayks, speshly my
hand. i never kilt a guy bifoar. i lift the gun, breev in hold my breff
consentrait fink how this guy neal on my back wile Mick ram my
face in the muck. no shayks now. sqeez. Bang!!! Del gun jumps. the
guy face hits the wall in front ov him noyze lyke splitting happel and

4 **handy**: ready to use   7 **sept** = except   14 **do sb. over** (infml): attack and beat sb.
17 **rabbit on about sth.**: talk about unimportant things   20 **sunup**: time when the
sun rises   21 **payshent** = patient ['peɪʃnt]: able to wait for a long time   29 **happel**
= apple

he slydes down leeving blod on the brix. no sownd. jus slyding down and this little hoal lyke belly button in his back.

wen i fire, this ovver guy yell owt Pete – hey Pete wot you shooting at? i duck down say noffing. Pete say noffing 2 – firs tyme in his lyfe probly. the guy yell owt again Pete hey Pete. i stay hid.  5 after a minit stoans rattel and futsteps running. i luck owt, see the guy running souf lyke the clappers.

Noffing more 2 tel. I tutch Pete wiv my foot. he wont neal on no 1 elses back. i wolkit acrost the street, luck norf. No Subbys. Mebbe thay dint get kickowt after all. mebbe old Pete got it rong. i bet he  10 fink so.

i go souf, hoam 4 brake fast.

Wear you bin our Daz, sez Mam.

no wear Mam, I sez.

thats jus wear you sed you was going, she sez.  15

shes dry, our mam.

---

1 **brix** = bricks: *Backsteine*   2 **belly button** (infml): *Bauchnabel*

# ZOE

Another sleepless night, and I must've changed my mind a hundred 39
times as the hours dragged by.

Put yourself in my place. You love your parents but you've
decided to leave forever without even saying goodbye. You're gonna
5  do it tomorrow, so this is your last night in the bed you've slept in all
your life. You're going out under a trash truck, and any one of four
things might happen. You might be seen getting under, in which
case the whole thing's blown. You might succeed in getting under,
but be spotted at the gate. If that happens the crew dies and they put
10 you away someplace you'll never get out of. If you make it through
the gate you might lose your hold as the truck speeds along the
freeway, in which case you're dead. Or you might succeed and find
yourself without food or shelter in a bleak and alien world.

Would that help you sleep?

15   Anyway, morning comes and I have to act normal. I feel like the
condemned guy must feel, eating a breakfast that'll never get digested
because in less than an hour he'll be dead. Unreal's the word, I guess.
Or detached.

There we sit, the three of us, eating cornflakes, as usual, and
20 Mum says something like, 'I've packed everything we won't need
before Friday. Have you called the telephone company yet?'

And Dad says, 'I'll do it from the office, first thing.' He's sold the
business and is tying up loose ends.

Mum looks at me. 'Be sure to remind Mrs Corrigan about your
25 file, Zoe. They'll want it at your new school.'

'Okay, Mum,' I say. My breakfast's choking me but when will I eat
cornflakes again?

Dad's leaving. To keep from bursting into tears I think about how
he sold our home without even telling me. I grip my spoon and stare

---

8 **blow sth.** (infml): make sth. known that was a secret   16 **condemn** [kən'dem]:
(zum Tode) verurteilen   **digest**: verdauen   18 **detached**: showing a lack of feeling
23 **tie up loose ends** [luːs]: deal with all the remaining details of sth.

into my bowl and keep thinking about that till the sound of his car fades away. Even then I have to blink back some tears but my head's down and Mum doesn't notice.

I mumble that I'm not hungry, push my bowl away and leave the kitchen. In my room I sit on my bed (last time here) and weep. I do 5 it as quietly as I can, though my parents never come in without asking. I feel I could cry forever, but I have to make it look like I'm going to school.

I pick up my stuff and go downstairs. My eyes are red but that's okay – Mum knows I'm upset we're leaving. She's doing the dishes. I 10 can hear her at the sink. I can't go in there. I know if I do I'll abandon my plan. I conjure up a picture of Daz, put on my anorak with the big pockets, call out, 'Bye, Mum,' and leave (forever) through the front door.

Wednesdays, the trucks work the commercial section. I pedal 15 that way. It's eight forty-five and lots of other people are going that way too, but none of them are kids. There's no school near the commercial section. I feel conspicuous. If Pohlman's having me tailed they'll pick me up for sure. At the first intersection I turn off and make for one of the supermarkets. Crossing an overgrown 20 vacant lot I dump my bike and books and other schoolstuff. It feels like a decisive step. No turning back.

There was this story in all the papers oh – two years ago. A Chippy, Dred fanatic, rode into Fairlawn Suburb in broad daylight under a trash truck. Suicide mission. Sprayed a shopping mall with 25 machinegun fire till the bouncers cut him down. Sixteen, seventeen people died. Anyway the papers printed a diagram showing how the guy rode the truck, and that's how I'm going out.

In the supermarket I buy stuff I can carry in my pockets. Stuff Chippies can't get, or can't get easily, like cigarettes and fancy soap 30

---

11 **abandon sth.**: stop doing sth.    12 **conjure sth. up**: make sth. appear as a picture in your mind    18 **conspicuous**: easy to see or notice    19 **tail sb.**: follow sb. closely, esp. in order to watch where they go    22 **decisive**: very important 25 **suicide**: act of killing yourself    26 **cut sb. down** (infml): kill sb.

and coffee. I buy a lipstick and a compact and a tin of Germolene and some aspirin and a box of candy. I get butter and cheese and salami. I make my selection thoughtfully, with Daz's mother in mind. It's a sort of bribe. I spend quite a lot of my savings but I hang onto
5 some too, aware that the most precious commodity of all out there is cash.

I check out at nine thirty and the road to the commercial section is a lot quieter. All of the buildings that make up the section are similar – long, low structures of glass and concrete, severe and
10 functional but well spaced with smooth lawns and tidy flowerbeds between. Today the flowerbeds have that depressing, washed-up look you get in early November so they match my mood exactly.

I see a trash truck right away, but the sound the trash makes going in tells me it's still almost empty, with a long way to go. I walk
15 on, taking care to steer well clear of the block where Dad has his office.

I find what I'm looking for at ten past ten. The truck is parked up between two factory units and the four-man crew is leaning on a wall, taking a break. I walk past. The guys are smoking, chewing the
20 fat. None of them looks in my direction. Beyond their line of vision I turn left and walk toward the door of the building, hoping nobody's watching me through the windows of tinted glass. Instead of going to the door I turn left again and walk along the front of the factory to the corner. Here I flatten myself against the wall and take a peek. If
25 DS are watching now, they'll have me for sure. Maybe I'm half hoping they will.

The truck's about four metres away, between me and the crew. By looking under the vehicle I can see their feet. I glance around. A pickup is cruising up the street. I lean on the wall and pretend I'm

---

1 **compact** ['- -]: small flat box with a mirror and powder that women use
**Germolene**: antiseptic cream    4 **bribe** (n): *Bestechungsmittel*    5 **commodity**: thing
that is useful    9 **concrete** (n) ['- -]: *Beton*    **severe** [sɪ'vɪə]: extremely plain without
any decoration    10 **smooth**: flat and even, not rough    12 **match sth.**: go well
together    **mood**: way you are feeling at a particular time    15 **steer clear of sth.**:
avoid sth. because it may cause problems    19–20 **chew the fat** (infml): have a
long friendly talk with sb.

fixing a hangnail till it goes by. Then I take a deep breath and walk to
the truck, praying no crewman sees my feet, and duck under. In the
shadow I crouch motionless, my hair touching the caked, oily dirt
under the truck. If DS have been watching, surely now's the moment
they'll strike? Seconds pass and there's no shout, no pounding feet.    5
Am I relieved or disappointed? I dunno. I breathe out slowly, looking
for the brackets it showed in that diagram, hoping the crew's break
won't end just yet. I spot them – eight flat strips of steel which fasten
the truck's side-guards to the chassis. They cross at forty-five degrees
the right angle between the side-guard and the underneath of the    10
truck. There are four of them on each side. They're about three feet
apart, and I find I can easily wrap my arms round one and swing my
legs up through the next so that the strip is hooked behind my
knees. The trouble is that this leaves me very close to the side, so
that anybody glancing between the slats of the side-guard will be    15
sure to see me hanging like a sloth. Still, it's a good secure position
and the best I can manage.

I dangle. If you think I'm not scared, you're crazy. I'm terrified.
It's not the danger of being spotted so much as the thought of what
it'll be like when the truck starts moving. I mean okay, it's been done    20
before, but that guy knew he was going to die anyway and I'm no
Dred fanatic.

Presently, the crew decides to move, and I'm in luck. We've no
more calls to make. The vehicle bounces a bit but we're headed
straight for the nearest gate. My butt's clearing the cement by about    25
four inches and there's a terrific sense of speed. To take my mind off
this I turn my head to the right and peer through the slats. We've
cleared the commercial section and are passing through a leafy
residential part. Pedestrians walk dogs and push strollers within six
feet of me but nobody looks at the truck. I pray to God to send us no    30
red lights, and we get none.

---

1 **hangnail**: *Niednagel*    3 **crouch**: put your body close to the ground by bending
your legs under you    9 **side-guard**: *Seitenschutz (Gitter)*    **chassis** ['ʃæsi]: frame
that a vehicle is built on    15 **slat**: *(Gitter-)Stab*    16 **sloth**: *Faultier*    28 **leafy**:
having a lot of trees and plants    29 **stroller**: buggy

For some reason, now that it's actually happening I don't feel nearly so bad as I did earlier. Adrenalin, I guess.

At the gate there's no hassle at all. I'm amazed. We stop, but the bouncer doesn't even leave his kiosk. He just yells something to the
5  crewboss who yells something back, the pole goes up and we're through. We cruise along the freeway. I'd pictured myself, if I ever got this far, clinging on for dear life as the jolting flung me this way and that, threatening to break the tenuous hold of my aching arms on some greasy gismo. Forget it. The jolting's minimal till we turn off
10  the freeway, and it's only minutes to the dump from there.

At the dump three of the men get out and walk off, leaving the crewboss to dump the trash. While he's doing that, leaning out the cab and looking back, I roll out on his blind side and get down behind a mound. It stinks, but I'm out.
15  And that's how easy it is. Of course, they're not looking for people breaking out. I mean, what Subby in her right mind would choose to be a Chippy?

---

8 **tenuous**: so weak that it hardly exists   9 **greasy**: covered in oil   **gismo** (also **gizmo**, infml): *Dingsbums*   13 **blind side**: direction in which sb. cannot see very much   14 **mound**: small hill   16 **in your right mind**: not crazy

# DAZ

40   i dint get no sleap that nite even thogh i wos nackert. 2 worid, see.
that Pete 1 ov Cal guys and i kiltim. also it com reel cowld and the
wind blue the polifeen sheat down of the broken windo. i after get
up and fixit and wen i go back 2 bed i cant get warm even wiv
2 coats over.                                                                5

Wensday morning our Mam fynd all the tucker stamps gon. ear
our Daz she sez wears all the bleedin stamps. i canot tel a lye our
Mam i sez (not much i cant) it wos me.

she giv me el. i after take it. i feal roten alreddy and she maykit
wors. owm i spos 2 fead the 2 ov us wivowt stamps she sez. dunno   10
Mam i sez. no she sez neever do i.

no brake fast, plus she send me owt in the cowld 2 deel stamps or
tucker. How do i know wear is deelas Wensday morning? i take Del
gun witch is all i got to deel and hang abowt, aster cupple guys,
finely pickup this hardloaf bred and lengf ov sossidge witch the    15
sossidge probly dog. After handover Del gun and the guy wont frow
in no coffee neever the tite git. Me and Mam eat the bred and sossidge
and i dont find no collar init witch is 1 big serprize.

bigger serprize coming thogh.

---

3 **polifeen** = polythene: Polyäthylen   9 **give sb. hell** (infml): give sb. a hard time
10 **owm i** = how am I   17 **tight git** (sl): *geiziger Widerling*

# ZOE

When the truck moved off I stayed down. With the actual escape ⟦41⟧
behind me my mind was free for the first time to contemplate the
enormity of the step I had taken, and I found myself overwhelmed
by a combination of emotions, the strongest of which were regret,
5  sheer disbelief and rising panic. It was as much as I could do to stop
myself jumping up and running after the truck, begging to be taken
back. I stuffed my handkerchief in my mouth, closed my eyes and
fought for the control which alone could help me now.

I don't know how long I stayed there. I know that gradually
10  I became aware that I was terribly cold, and that the cry of gulls was
everywhere. I pulled the wadded handkerchief from my mouth,
wiped my face with it and thrust it into a pocket with the aspirin and
the cigarettes.

I was shaking. Stop it, I said to myself. Stop this right now, Zoe,
15  or you're finished. You're here. This is real. Regret's worse than
useless and panic'll get you killed.

I raised myself a little and looked over the mound. Three, four
hundred yards away some guys were working, sorting stuff into
piles. A little way beyond them was a track, and beyond that was
20  open ground, covered with weeds and scrub. There seemed to be no
fence round the dump – nothing to stop me getting up and just
walking away. I didn't do it, though, because I had no idea what the
guys' reaction would be if a Subby kid suddenly materialised among
them. What would they do – kill me? They might. Nobody'd ever
25  know. They could belt me over the head and make a hole and plant
me and I'd be gullfeed – part of the dump.

I looked around. Off to my left was where the trucks checked in –
a little hut beside a muddy track. As I watched, a truck drew up and

---

4 **regret** (n): feeling of sadness because of sth. that you have done   5 **disbelief**:
feeling of not being able to believe sth.   19 **pile**: number of things that have been
placed on top of each other   **track**: a rough path or road   20 **scrub**: small bushes
and trees   23 **materialise**: appear suddenly   25 **belt sb.** (infml): hit sb. hard

a man came out of the hut and stood, talking to the driver. Not that way, then. Directly behind me were great drifts of garbage. It was impossible to know what lay beyond them, so I looked to my right. A track marked the boundary of the dump in that direction too, but it must be at least a quarter of a mile away. There were no vehicles, 5 though, and no people I could see. I was in jeans and anorak. If I got up and walked that way without hurrying, maybe nobody would notice me. One thing was certain – if I stayed where I was I'd either be discovered or I'd freeze to death. I stood up and started walking.

Nobody shouted. The guys who were sorting went right on doing 10 it, and the man by the hut continued to talk to the driver. I plodded on with my head down in imitation of the Chippy's dejected gait. I was walking away from the city but that was all right – once off the dump I could circle round, and it was only eleven thirty.

I made it to the track with muddy shoes, but no trouble. I began 15 to circle the dump clockwise, watching out for people. When I saw the little hut in front of me I made a detour through the scrub, not returning to the track till I'd left it way behind. When I'd walked a half-circle there was a road, half choked with weeds, which seemed to go toward the city. I turned on to it and after that I didn't see 20 anybody for quite a while. I plodded on, looking for the tallest block in town.

* * *

It's a bit vague, the tallest block in town. If I'd had any idea this was going to happen the last time I saw Daz, I'd have got the street and his apartment number. And if I'd had more time I'd have done some 25 other things, too. I'd have worked out a way to take some of my warmest clothing with me for a start. As it was I only thought how I'd need both hands free to hold on to that truck, and so I'd brought nothing that wouldn't go in my pockets. I could've worn some extra

11 **plod**: walk slowly with heavy steps    12 **dejected**: unhappy and disappointed
**gait**: way of walking    17 **detour** ['diːtʊə]: a longer route that you take to avoid a
problem or visit a place    19 **choked**: blocked

things as a way of getting them out but I hadn't. In short, this had to be the worst-organised expedition ever mounted.

The weeds thinned out as I approached the city. I was passing between broken buildings now, and I began to see people. First there
5 were some little kids in the ruins. I guess ruins make neat places to play if you're a kid. This bunch were standing in a ring, laughing and poking with sticks at something on the ground. I didn't look their way because I didn't want to attract their attention, but as I drew level one of them, a tiny, dirty-nosed girl called out, 'Hey
10 missus, come see what we got.' I pretended not to hear, but then the others started calling and I was scared their noise might bring people so I went over.

It was a dead man. They'd found a dead man and filled his nose, mouth and one ear with twigs and grass stems. They'd removed his
15 boots. A little boy was wearing them round his neck. If this'd been Silverdale I'd have shooed the kids away and called a cop. Here, I was at a loss. I said, 'This poor man is dead. You should tell somebody – an adult, not be fooling around like this.' They gazed at me as if I was something from another galaxy, and the biggest boy –
20 the one with the boots – eyed me shrewdly and said, 'He's ours, missus. We found him. You wanna buy his doodies?'

Doodies is Chippy for clothes. I shook my head.

'Boots?' He lifted them so I could see the soles. 'Good boots for your fella. Goin' for peanuts.'
25 'I – I don't have –.'

'Stamps, then. Gimme stamps.'

I'd been about to say I had no fella. He thought I had no cash. I shook my head again. 'Look, I don't want – you shouldn't be doing this. This is a corpse. You can get diseases. All sorts of nasty things.
30 What would your parents –?' I didn't know what I was saying, really. I just wanted out of there.

---

2 **mount sth.** (v): organize sth.   16 **shoo sb. sway**: make a sound that tells sb.
to go away   20 **shrewd**: clever   29 **corpse**: dead body

The boy peered at me through red-rimmed, narrow eyes. 'You –
you Subby, encha?'

His companions regarded me now with a fresh interest. I nodded.
'Yes. That is, I was. Not anymore. I ran away. Do you know a boy – a
man, called Daz?'

He eyed me scornfully, ignoring my question. 'Ran away?' He
laughed, jeeringly. 'Gerraway, missus. Subbies don't run away. You
kickout, right?'

I shook my head. 'No. I ran away. D'you know a man called Daz?
He wears a black leather jacket.'

'Black leather granny! You kickout, encha? Wanna place? Gimme
peanuts, I show you a place. Good place. Dry.' He grinned, thrusting
out a grubby palm.

I shook my head once more and turned away. Behind unbroken
cloud the sun was falling westward. I knew if I didn't find Daz before
dark something would happen to me. Watching these kids had
convinced me of that. They were just little kids, but they looked and
behaved like rats. Thin, darting, glitter-eyed rats. If they'd known
what was in my pockets I think they'd have killed me for it, small as
they were. I hurried away and their cries pursued me. Kickout, they
shrilled. Kickout, kickout, kickout.

\* \* \*

I was now approaching the centre of Grandma's beloved Rawhampton, or what was left of it. I'd spotted a very tall building some
minutes before and was hurrying toward it in the hope that it would
turn out to be Daz's block. I'd seen a bit of the town from Ned Volsted's car the night we went chippying, but it'd been practically dark,
and anyway you don't see things all that well from a car. That brief
glimpse certainly hadn't prepared me for the panorama of desolation
which now unfolded around me.

---

6 **scornful**: *verächtlich*    7 **jeer** (v): laugh at sb. to show that you do not respect
them    **gerraway** = get away (BE, infml): used to show that you do not believe
what sb. has said    12 **thrust**: *ausstrecken*    13 **grubby**: dirty    **palm**: inner surface
of the hand

The streets were cracked and broken and littered with every sort of debris. Long puddles of foul, stagnant water lay in gutters clogged with filth. Here and there sat the rusting carcasses of cars and trucks, completely stripped and without their wheels. Some were evidently 5 in use as dwellings, because I saw makeshift curtains strung over glassless windows and signs of life behind them. And these weren't the worst places. Among the rubble of smashed and burned-out buildings, people had made shanties out of crates and plastic sacks and cardboard boxes. Little fires smouldered before some of these 10 and listless children huddled in the smoke, poking the flames with sticks. There was an unpleasant smell, strong in some places, faint in others, but always there.

I'd just begun to think every building in the city must be derelict when I came to a row of little shops. Plate glass windows gleamed 15 dully behind heavy-gauge wire mesh, and there were crudely painted signs above. One said **RUDY'S DOODIE'S – bought and sold – cash stamp's xchange**. Another said **TUCKER – savage dog on gard**. A small, home-made handcart stood outside this shop and in the cart, swaddled in rags, lay a baby.

20 As I gazed around, the enormity of the step I had taken began to dawn and I wondered whether, if I were to run all the way back to the dump and get under a truck, I might get back into Silverdale before anyone realised I'd gone.

It was pure fantasy and I knew it, but a sort of panic was growing 25 in me and my mind was searching frantically for something to keep it from snapping. I knew if I dwelt on my situation now I'd start screaming, and that if I screamed forever it wouldn't change a thing. With a terrific effort I tore my mind away from thoughts of undoing what could never be undone, and walked on into how things really 30 are.

---

2 **debris** (fml) ['debri]: pieces of material that are not wanted    **puddle**: *Pfütze*
**stagnant**: not moving    **gutter**: *Rinnstein*    **clog sth.**: block sth.    3 **carcass**: *Wrack*
5 **dwelling**: house or flat    **makeshift** (adj): improvised   8 **shanty**: small hut where
very poor people live   9 **smoulder**: burn slowly without a flame   15 **heavy-gauge**:
strong    **wire mesh**: *Maschendraht*   19 **swaddle**: wrap in clothes    **rags**: dirty and
torn clothes

\* \* \*

How things really are. Daz had told me he lived with his mother in an apartment, and like you do I'd formed pictures in my mind of what I imagined his mother and the apartment would look like. They were nothing fancy, these imaginary pictures. I'd seen apartment blocks and a selection of their inhabitants through the windows 5 of Ned's car, and of course I'd been fed all my life with stories about how Chippies live. I knew I wasn't about to walk into some antiseptic glass palace and meet a beautifully turned-out matron whom Daz would introduce as his mother, but I'd no idea how bad it would actually be. 10

From the outside, the block was like the ones I'd seen. There were the usual damp-stained walls and broken, boarded-over windows, and the usual knot of dirty, red-eyed kids round the doorway. It was when I got through the doorway things started to get heavy. 15

I mentioned a smell before – the one that was strong in some places and faint in others. Well, that was the first thing that hit me, and I do mean hit. I was in a dim lobby with a cement floor and rough plaster walls that were covered with graffiti. In front of me was a flight of cement stairs and an elevator. I could tell by just looking 20 at it the elevator hadn't worked in a long, long time. The floor felt sticky under my shoes and there were puddles and piles of trash in corners. I nearly gagged on the smell. The kids, squealing and chattering, had come in after me. Their voices echoed in the bleak lobby and they plucked at my clothes. 25

'Daz,' I asked. 'Does Daz live here?' A small boy jerked his head toward the stairs. 'Free up.'

'Thanks.'

---

8 **be well turned out** (infml): be well dressed    12 **damp** (n): state of being slightly wet    **board sth. up**: cover a window, door, etc. with wooden boards    19 **plaster**: Putz    23 **gag on sth.**: have the unpleasant feeling in your mouth and stomach as if you have to vomit    23 **squeal**: make a long high sound    25 **pluck at sth.**: hold sth. with the fingers and pull it gently

The half-landing windows were boarded up so the stairway was dark and I kept stepping on squashy things I couldn't see. There seemed to be four apartments on the first floor, but only one had a door, so maybe the others were unoccupied. On the next floor two
5  apartments had doors. A fierce-sounding dog threw itself against the inside of one just as I was passing.

All of the third-floor apartments had doors. I stopped by one that had the number eleven painted on it, and knocked. Some of the kids had followed me up. They stood on the stairs, watching me through
10  rusty iron rails. I heard footsteps, and a voice, suspicious, called, 'Yeah?' I knew that voice.

'It's me, Daz. Zoe.' A bolt scraped, the door flew open and we were in each other's arms.

\* \* \*

We were in a little hallway that had the same cement floor as the
15  landing outside, only cleaner. Not clean, but cleaner. The walls had once been yellow, but damp must've got in, and now the paint was curled and blistered and flakes of it lay on the floor. There was a smell like toadstools. Four doors led off this hallway, one in front of me and three on my left. The one straight ahead was open and led to
20  a kitchen. When Daz closed the outer door the only light came from there.

Daz took my hand and led me to the last door on the left. As he opened it he called out, 'Hey, Mam, look – we got a visitor.' The forced cheerfulness was transparent and I felt like I was walking into
25  an ogre's lair.

Scattered across the floor were bits and pieces of matting and threadbare carpet. Apart from these the room contained only an iron

---

2 **squashy**: soft and easy to crush   4 **unoccupied**: empty   5 **fierce**: angry and aggressive   12 **bolt**: *Riegel*   17 **curled**: *gewellt*   **blistered**: *Blasen werfend*
18 **toadstool**: kind of mushroom   25 **ogre**: a cruel man-eating giant   **lair**: place where a wild animal sleeps or hides   26 **scattered**: spread over a wide area
27 **threadbare**: old and thin because it has been used a lot

stove whose chimney went out through a window, and two chairs, one each side of the stove. The chairs were saggy, colourless arm-chairs and in one of them sat a woman who might have been made to match. With a son like Daz she couldn't have been much more than forty-five, but she looked at least seventy. She was wearing a lumpy green cardigan over a black, turtleneck sweater and a long grey skirt with a ragged hem. Her thin legs were bare except for blue ankle socks and her feet were encased in what looked like a man's broken boots. Grey hair hung in greasy rattails to her shoulders. White bony fingers gripped the armrests of her chair and she gazed at her son with lustreless eyes.

'Visitor? What you on about, our Daz? Who is it?'

'I'm Zoe, Mrs –.' I broke off. I didn't know her name. I'd run away from home to be with someone whose name I didn't even know.

Daz said, 'This is Zoe, Mam. She's a – she's from Silverdale. She'll be staying here awhile.'

'Staying?' The woman leaned forward. 'A Subby lass, staying here? Have you gone barmy, lad? D'you want to get us both topped? How'd she get out of Silverdale anyway?'

'Under a trashtruck,' I said. 'I rode out under a trashtruck.'

'Aye, and what you done, that's what I'd like to know. What they want you for in Silverdale, eh?'

'Nothing. I haven't done anything, Mrs –. I ran away to be with Daz.'

'Daz? What's our Daz got to do with you?' She looked at her son.

'Only one reason Subbies run. They done something, see? DS wants 'em. She stays here, place'll be crawling with lornorders 'fore you can turn round. Get her out of here, son. Get rid of her.'

Daz looked from me to her. 'I can't, Mam. Where's she supposed to go – out on the street? Anyway, I love her.'

'Love?' The woman laughed wheezily. 'You telling me you fell for a Subby girl after what they did to our Del? Forgot, did you?'

---

2 **saggy**: *durchgesessen*   6 **turtleneck sweater**: *Rollkragenpullover*   7 **hem**: *Saum*
8 **encase sth.** (fml): surround sth. completely, esp. to protect it   9 **rattail**: *Ratten-schwanz (Frisur)*   11 **lustreless**: not shining   17 **lass** (infml): girl   31 **wheezy**: *schnaufend*

He shook his head. 'No, Mam. I didn't forget. I've never forgotten our Del, have I? Wanted to join Dred and get 'em back, only you weren't that keen, were you?'

'Huh! Wouldn't have you now, though, would they? Subby-lover
5 they'd call you, and they'd be right. Anyway she can't stay here. I want no raids on this house, we've trouble enough.'

I know what you're thinking. You're thinking this old lady's hospitality stinks, but she was right. They execute Chippies who harbour fugitives or kidnap people, and I'd come here thoughtlessly,
10 expecting to be taken in. I realised now what I'd done, and if there'd been anywhere else for me to go – anywhere at all – I'd have walked out, but there wasn't. Death was waiting outside, and so I had to stand there while Daz and bis mother fought over me.

In the end they compromised. The old lady said that since it was
15 dark now I'd better stay till morning. Daz winked at me. I guess he thought his mother would relent tomorrow and everything would be fine. I wasn't so sure.

With that and missing my family, I'd have spent a lousy night if they'd put me in a feather bed. A damp mattress on the floor and a
20 coat to cover me left me no chance. My feet were like chilled mutton and I think I cried all night.

\* \* \*

Barraclough, their name is. The old lady told me at breakfast. She's different in the mornings because that's when she pops her pill. She's got something Chippies call the dulleye, which I guess is depression,
25 and she's on pills for it.

Breakfast was at 8 a.m. It was hot, watery coffee and hard bread. Daz and his mother dunked their bread in the coffee so I did too.

---

6 **raid on sth.** (n): a surprise visit by the police looking e.g. for illegal goods
8 **hospitality**: friendly and generous behaviour towards guests    15 **wink at sb.**:
close one eye and open it again quickly    16 **relent**: finally agree to sth. after
refusing    20 **mutton**: meat from a fully grown sheep    27 **dunk sth. in sth.**:
put food quickly into liquid before eating it

Afterwards Daz told me the bread was a special treat because I was there – usually they just have the coffee.

They don't talk over breakfast, the Barracloughs. I sat there trying to eat wet bread without slurping, saying Darren Barraclough over and over in my head. Darren Barraclough. I like it. I think it has a 5 ring to it. I needed to find things I liked that morning.

They don't talk over breakfast, but we talked straight after. The old lady's pill saved me from having to leave right away but it didn't blunt her sense of reality. She started asking me questions. Did my parents know anything about Daz. What did I say to them when I 10 left the house. Had I left a note. What time yesterday would they have started to worry. When would they have known I was definitely missing. What would they do then. Had I relatives or friends in Silverdale I might be with. In other suburbs. Would they get the police in right away. What did I think they'd think had happened to me. 15

I did my best to answer. She and Daz knew the authorities would be looking for me, and that sooner or later they'd widen their search to include the city. I said, 'The city's a big place to find one person in. Surely if I stay indoors till they get tired looking it'll be okay?'

Daz shook his head. 'You were seen, Zoe, yesterday. The kids you 20 told me about, and them downstairs. Others. You were dirty from the dump but even the little kids had you sussed. Lornorders pay for information and there's a lot of hungry people out there. Soon as the law comes sniffing around, someone'll finger you.'

'Then what can we do, Daz? What do I do? I don't want to bring 25 the police down an you, but I don't know any place outside of Silverdale other than this.'

'I know. Listen. I have to go out for a while. See a guy.' He stood, pulling on his jacket. 'I've got an idea but I don't know if I can swing it. You stay here with Mam and don't even stick your nose outside.' 30 He turned in the doorway, grinning. 'And if you hear a fan, stay away from the window.'

---

4 **slurp**: make a loud noise while you are drinking sth.   9 **blunt sth.**: make sth. weaker or less effective   22 **have sb. sussed**: understand sb.   24 **finger sb.** (infml): accuse sb. of doing sth. illegal and tell the police about it   29 **swing sth.** (infml): *etwas schaukeln, etwas hinkriegen*

# DAZ

Zoe wiv me now and evryfing shoud be grate but is not. i watch her    42
in the partmen. she lucking at fings and i can see she dont lykem.
any ovver Subby i be glad, fink ah well now you see how it is but not
wiv Zoe. i wish ther coud be somfing Zoe lyke but we got noffing.
5  i always new that but it never feal so bad lyke now. i fink if Subbys'd
let her back she go and i never see her again. i howld her hand and
she make a littel smile but not happy.
   Oh Zoe i do anifing 2 make you happy. wolk a fousan myle. slap
Cal mouf.
10   anifing.

*Zoe is the centre of his life!*

*His love is so big*

# ZOE

**43**  So there I was, alone with the old lady. The pill was working and she
was okay with me, but still and all I knew I wasn't welcome and
that's a bad feeling.

I thought the stuff I'd brought might make it better so I got my
anorak and emptied the pockets on to the table. She sat and watched, 5
saying nothing. I'd hoped her face might light up or something but
it didn't. When everything was on the table I said, 'This stuff's for
you. I hope you can use it.' She looked at it for a minute and then
she said, 'Is this all you brought?' I felt a stab of anger. Here I was
trying to be friends with her, giving her stuff she'd probably never 10
seen in her life and all she could do was criticise because I hadn't
brought more. I looked at her, 'What d'you mean, all? Can you get
stuff like this, even in small quantities?'

She shook her head. 'Didn't mean that, girl. This house never saw
such goodies. What I mean is, where's your clothes? Shoes? The stuff 15
you're wearing won't last forever, y'know, and you can't just go to the
store and buy more like you could in Silverdale.' She nodded at the
food and things. 'You better hang on to that – it'll get you strong
shoes and a change of underwear, but you'd have done better to
bring them along in the first place.' 20

She really put me down. I'd planned to offer my little store of
cash, too, but she'd only tell me I was going to need it, which was
true. 'Look,' I said. 'I had to leave in a hurry. I had no time to plan,
but I thought it'd be nice to bring along some of the stuff you can't
get here, that's all.' 25

To my surprise she leant across the table and squeezed my arm.
'It was a nice thought, only –.' Tears glittered in the creases at the
corners of her eyes. 'Can you imagine my face with lipstick? This
face? And what's the use of being clean and smelling nice for a week
if you've got to go back to –.' 30

---

9 **stab of sth.**: sudden pain or unpleasant feeling    21 **put sb. down** (infml): make
sb. look or feel stupid    27 **crease** (n): line in the skin

She broke off and got up, gathering the three chipped mugs. I followed her out to the kitchen. I know it's silly, but I expected she'd run hot water into the sink, squirt in some washing-up liquid, wash the mugs and hand them over hot and steamy for me to wipe.

5 There was a sink. A stainless steel one, but like the elevator you only had to see it to know it hadn't been used in a long time. Its taps were dry and rusted and a foul smell rose from its drain. On a worktop beside it stood a battered plastic bucket with water in it. The water looked grey and scummy and Mrs Barraclough did the

10 mugs in it, dipping them quickly and standing them upside down on the drainer. I looked around for something to wipe with and she said, 'Leave 'em, they'll dry.'

'Where d'you get the water?' I asked.

'Raintank on the roof.'

15 'But it doesn't come through your taps?'

'No. Folks'd waste it if it did. You gotta go up for it.'

'Can I get some now?'

'No. You heard Daz. You gotta stay out of sight, and anyway we've got our ration for today.'

20 'That?' I nodded at the bucket.

'That for washing. This to drink.' She opened a sliding door under the sink to reveal a second bucket, threequarters full. For some reason it reminded me I needed to go to the john. I mentioned it and she said 'Well – I was beginning to think Subbies must've

25 found a way to do without. Second door.'

Oh, you needn't worry. I'm not going to dwell on it. If I tell you the Barracloughs have three plastic buckets in all, you've probably got the picture.

When I returned to the kitchen, she'd left it, and I was about to

30 go back to the living room when I heard a familiar sound. I looked out the window, leaning across the sink to do it. There were high buildings all round so you couldn't see much sky, but the noise grew and I saw a fan go over, low. I ducked back, though the window was

---

3 **squirt**: *(heraus)spritzen*    4 **wipe sth.**: (here) dry sth.    6 **tap**: *Wasserhahn*
7 **drain**: *Abflussrohr*    9 **scummy**: dirty

so dirty I doubt a pigeon on the sill could've seen me. As the fan's engine faded I heard a siren not far off and a minute later a copcar went by, travelling fast.

The old lady was back in her armchair. The pill must've been wearing off because she glowered at me as I came in the room.　5

'Hear that?' She nodded toward the street. 'They're looking for you, girl. If that boy don't hurry you're back in Silverdale and we're dead.'

I couldn't think of anything to say. I sat in the other chair and we stared at the stove, avoiding each other's eyes.　10

---

1 **pigeon** ['pɪdʒɪn]: *Taube*　5 **glower at sb.** ['glæʊə]: look at sb. in an angry way

# DAZ

wots the rottenest feeling?                                                    `44`
    scairt? no
    hungry? no
    cold? no
5    loanly? no
    sick? no
    ashamed ov yor movver, ashamed ov yor hoam. that's wot.

* * *

i tecka big chanse go up the school see Mister James. I disser pointim
but he like me just the same. hes teeching. i wayt. braketyme he
10 coms owt sez wot you doing hear Barraclough you xpelt. i com rite
owt wiv it. you in FAIR Mister James i sez.

    he goes wite. goes shush. lucks all rownd. howd you know that
he sez. i larf. fings, i sez. fings you say fings you do. just then a fan
coms over lo and he damnear fills his pants.

15    wot you want he sez. mebbe he finks i com 2 black male him or
somfing.

    want you 2 hyde some 1 i sez.

    hide some 1 he sez. hoo.

    girl i sez. Subby girl. name dont matter.

20    Subby girl he sez. i cant hyde no subby girl. thay catch me, i get
kickowt Silverdale. Mister James liv in Silverdale come 2 town
5 daze a weak.

    you wont get court i sez. lornoders wont luck in school cos you
Subby.

25    thay mite he sez. thay know i'm sim pafetick.

    if you sim pafetick i sez you hyde her. Mam and me get topt if
you dont. i hear copcar syren, gotta get back.

---

15 **black male** = blackmail sb.: *jdn. erpressen*   25 **sim pafetick** = sympathetic
(towards sth.): showing that you approve of sb./sth. and are willing to support them

okay he sez bring her after dark i do wot i can but i cant hyde her long. a day or 2 at moast. fanks Mister James i sez.

going hoam i seen abowt 6 copcars plus the fan. fan gotta speeka on it. lornorder tell frou the speeka how Subby girl missing. hare color. wot cloaths she got on. all lyke that. big reward 4 any 1 turn   5 her in or giv informashun.

i go faster. You fink abowt gerrin topt, you go faster 2.

# ZOE

We must've sat the best part of an hour, listening. It's amazing how sound travels. The guys in the fan kept moving from place to place, hovering to do their spiel about me. They got closer and closer till the tinny voice seemed to be directly over us, then moved off. I felt a little better as the noise receded, but no matter where they went we could still hear them, and of course we both realised that at this very moment somebody – one of the kids from last night – might be leading a bunch of cops here. When footfalls sounded on the stairs we tensed up and our eyes met across the cold stove, and when the outer door opened I half-rose ready to run, though I don't know where I thought I'd run to.

It was Daz. He closed the room door and leaned against it, breathing hard.

'They're everywhere,' he gasped. 'In the sky, on the ground, underground for all I know. You'd think it was a king they were looking for.'

His mother looked at him. 'Any in this building?'

He shook his head. 'Not yet. Couple of cars in the next street.' He turned to me. 'Come on – I know a place you can hide till they've gone.'

I followed him out of the room, out of the apartment and down the twilit stairs. 'Daz,' I whispered. 'Where are you taking me?'

'Basement,' he said.

We passed the doorway we came in last night and went on down. It was totally dark and knee-deep in trash and it stank. Daz switched on a flashlight and led me toward an enormous old furnace. In the dark above it, pipes filled the ceiling space like spaghetti, but the air was cold and dank and I knew nobody had stoked *this* furnace in years. I knew what Daz had in mind too, and it crossed my mind

---

3 **spiel** (infml): long speech that sb. has used many times intended to persuade you to believe sth.   4 **tinny**: *blechern*   22 **twilit** ['twaɪlɪt]: *von der Abendsonne beschienen*
26 **furnace**: household heating system based on a boiler   28 **stoke sth.**: *etwas anheizen*

that this wasn't exactly the most original hiding place ever devised. In fact if I was a cop, it'd be one of the first places I'd look.

I'd underestimated him. He didn't open the door and tell me to get in. The furnace stood on a brick base, very close to the wall: so close that when he shone his torch on it I noticed that whoever had limewashed the walls down here back in the good old days hadn't been able to get at this section, which was black and greasy and furred with cobwebs.

'Halfway along there,' he said, 'there's a hole in the base. It's a crawl space, goes right in under the furnace.' He chuckled. 'I used to hide from our mam in there. I know it's not so nice, Zoe, but I want you to wait in there till I come back for you.'

He was right. It wasn't nice. I had to scrape along sideways and by the time I reached the hole my damp face was caked with cobwebs and flakes of rust and my hair was an old mop, stiff with dirt.

Under the furnace was horrible. Pitch black and horrible. I won't go on about it. I forced myself not to think about spiders and black beetles and thought about Daz as a little boy, hiding here from his mother. I wondered whether his brother Del had come here too, but that started me thinking about ghosts so I shook my head and thought about something else.

The cops came, eventually. I heard them on the stairs, then at the foot of the stairs where they paused to voice their disgust as flashlights showed the dirt they'd have to wade through in their shiny boots. I hoped it'd put them off: that their search would be perfunctory. I hoped one of them wouldn't turn out to be a Sherlock Holmes, the sort of guy who'd notice torn cobwebs and scuff marks in the dirt. I doubted it. My hidey-hole was a good one.

They didn't find me. They spent a minute, maybe a minute and a half in the place. They looked in the furnace – I heard the door

---

3 **underestimate sb.**: not realize how clever sb. is   8 **furred**: covered with sth. that looks like animal hair   10 **crawl space**: a space under the first floor or roof of a building that is not high enough to stand up in   14 **caked with**: covered with
18 **beetle**: *Käfer*   26 **perfunctory**: done as a duty without real interest   27 **scuff mark**: *Abriebstelle, Spur*   28 **hidey-hole** (infml): place where sb. hides

squeak – then one of them hit the boiler with something and the great hollow boom damn near creamed my brain, but that was all.

I listened as they went back up the stairs. After that it was just a matter of waiting for Daz to come. Wondering if he would, and what 5 I'd do if he didnt? Suppose he'd been arrested, and his mother too? Suppose they never came back – what then?

I was doing a pretty good job of driving myself crazy in that dark little hole when I heard his voice.

* * *

I was filthy all over, but he took me in his arms and hugged me. I felt 10 wonderful but I knew I didn't look it and I was glad he couldn't see me. I asked him what had happened with the cops.

'Routine search, Zoe. No tip-off, so they don't know I'm involved yet, but they will. Your old man must be loaded – they're offering big peanuts for you and somebody's gonna collect before long. That's 15 why we've got to get you out of here.'

'Yes, but where?'

'School.'

'School?'

'That's right.' He steered me toward the stairs and we climbed 20 stealthily up the four flights to the apartment. He went first, pressing himself against walls and peeping round corners, but all the doors were shut, the stairs and landings deserted. He turned and winked at me. 'Can't beat a visit from the law for making people stay home.'

Back in the apartment I had to visit that awful bucket again. Then 25 Daz sat me down and told me about the teacher, James. Mrs Barraclough was lying down so we had the room to ourselves. When he'd finished I said, 'Okay, so I hide in the school, but what happens to you when the cops get their tip-off – you and your mum?'

He shrugged. 'I dunno, Zoe. James said something about seeing a 30 guy, but I didn't know what he meant.' He chuckled. 'I don't think

---

2 **cream sth.** (infml): damage sth.    9 **filthy**: very dirty    12 **tip-off** (BE infml, AE: tip): secret information given e.g. to the police to warn them about sth. illegal
20 **stealthy**: doing things quietly or secretly

he knew himself, he was so scairt. We'll just have to see what happens.'

I spread my hands, palms up, on my knees and looked at them. They were filthy. So were my jeans. There were cobwebs all down the front of my jumper and I felt itchy. I remembered the bucket of  5 cold, scummy water in the kitchen and right then I'd have given anything to be standing in our gleaming shower back home. Tears filled my eyes and ran down my cheeks and I wiped at them with my fingers, knowing I was smearing dirt on my face. Daz got up and knelt by my chair and put his arms round me. He must've had a fair  10 idea why I was crying and he didn't say anything, just knelt there, rocking me in his arms like you would a little kid.

I hadn't been a Chippy very long but I was beginning to understand why Mrs Barraclough had to have those pills.

* * *

As soon as it was properly dark we set off for the school. I'd wanted  15 to clean myself up a bit before I went but Mrs Barraclough said I'd be safer the way I was. In fact, she persuaded me to take off my jumper, which was quite new, and put on an old one of hers which was through at the elbow and far too big for me. She had me take off my wristwatch and put it in my pocket. She thought people might  20 notice my shoes, too, but she was nowhere near my size so we decided I'd have to risk it. They were pretty messed up from the dump and anyway it was dark.

It was drizzling, too, and we didn't see many people as we trudged through the unlighted streets. The police always withdraw  25 to the suburbs at night so we didn't expect to encounter cops and we didn't. It was almost seven when we got to the school, which was housed in a low wooden building which stood by itself on the edge of a vast, derelict site. The place in darkness but the door was open, and as we let ourselves in the teacher hurried forward.  30

---

5 **itchy**: *juckend, kratzig*  24 **drizzle** (v): rain lightly  25 **trudge**: walk slowly or with heavy steps

'Anyone see you come in here, Barraclough?'

Daz shook his head. 'Don't think so, sir. This is Zoe. Zoe, this is Mister James who's gonna look after you.'

'Only for a day or so,' reminded the teacher. 'I'm taking a big risk,
5   y'know. If they find her here they'll close the school and strip me of my status.'

Daz chuckled. 'What's the matter, sir – don't you like it here? I thought you loved us Chippy kids. Wouldn't it be great to be near us all the time?'

10   The teacher shuddered. 'Heaven forbid. You'd better go now, Barraclough, but don't let anyone see you, and remember you've got to come up with a different arrangement for this young woman pretty soon.'

We embraced briefly and then he was gone. I followed the teacher
15   through the lobby, across the single classroom and into a tiny washroom. In this room stood a step-ladder, and a trapdoor in the ceiling was open.

James looked at me. 'Why a child like you should want to leave Silverdale to live in a place like this I don't know. What I do know is
20   this – that if I had my way I'd take you, by force if necessary, and restore you to your parents this very night.' He indicated the trapdoor. 'Climb through there. You'll find blankets, a flask of soup and a torch. It's the best I could manage. Use the torch only when absolutely necessary and be very quiet, especially during school
25   hours. All right?'

I nodded and said, 'You live in Silverdale, sir?'

'I do. Why'd you ask?'

'Well – I was wondering – I mean, could you get a message to my parents, tell them I'm alive and – you know?'

30   He smiled sadly, shaking his head. 'Your parents are frantic with grief, Zoe. What d'you think they'd do if I showed up with a message like that? D'you think they'd say, Oh fine – when you see her again, give her our best. D'you think they'd do that?'

---

5 **strip sb. of sth.**: take away sth. from sb. as a punishment   14 **embrace**: put your arms around sb.   21 **restore sb. to sth.**: bring sb. back to a former place **indicate**: point to sth.   31 **grief**: feeling of great sadness

I shook my head and he said. 'You're right, they wouldn't. They'd call DS and say There's a guy here knows where our child is, and DS would hang me by the thumbs till I told them where you were and who'd been hiding you, and then they'd go get young Barraclough and his widowed mother and hang them.'                    5

So that was that. He held the ladder and I climbed up. In the roofspace I found the things he'd mentioned, plus a couple of necessities he hadn't mentioned and I won't, either. And that's where I spent the next two days.

---

5 **be widowed**: have lost husband or wife

# DAZ

thay say trubble coms in 3s rite? 6s be mor lyk it. i leeve Zoe up the
school so trubble number 1 okay for a bit. don't get me rong –
i drather hav her wiv me enityme.

nex morning 2 lornorders com nokking. thay got a kid wiv em.
5 i open the doar. 1 ov em sez is this the guy and the kid sez yeah. you
can see by his face he finks he got his dirty littel pause on the peanuts
alreddy. wot guy i sez. wot you on abowt. Zoe May Askew sez the
cop. wear is she. hoo, i sez. never herd ov her i sez. this kid seen you
wiv her he sez. i luck at the kid. this kid, i sez. this kids the biggest
10 liar in town – say anifing 4 a peanut. thay push me asyde, start going
frou the place, opening doars, chucking fings abowt. or mam so
scairt she crys. i'm scairt 2 cos i remember Zoe jumper wot she swop
wiv our Mam. lornorders fynd it, we ded.

thay go frou the place lyke a hurry cane but dont find noffing. it
15 make em reely mad. 1 ov em sez lissen – we know she woz hear. you
hiding her somwear but we fynd her and wen we do you ded, boaf
ov you.

wen thay gon i sez 2 Mam wear Zoe jumper. shes just popt her
pill and she larfs. hear, she sez, and she pulls up her old jumper and
20 i see Zoe jumper undaneaf. yor a cool 1 Mam i sez. no she sez i'm a
warm 1 and she larfs again.

i dont know wear she gets em from.

* * *

Same day the lornorders com, rite? same day i'm wolking frou town
finking wot 2 do abowt Zoe wen i seen Mick coming tord me. Mick
25 dont tork 2 me no more, so i fink wen he sees me he mebbe cross
the road but he dont. insted he coms up 2 me and he sez Cal onto
you boy. wotcha mean i sez, finking its abowt Zoe. Pete, he sez.

---

1 **trouble comes in threes**: *ein Unglück kommt selten allein*   6 **pause** = paws (infml):
person's hands

i dont know no Pete, i sez, but my hart jump and he seen it in my
face. He larfs. You knowd him wel enuff 2 shootim, he sez. i dint
shoot no 1 i sez. i got no gun. lissen he sez. Pete shot wiv Del gun.
Cal knows cos Del gun always leave funny mark on shell and he
fownd the shell wot kilt Pete. Then a cuppla days ago a guy sells a    5
gun 2 Cal frend in the Diamond. Del gun, rite? Cal frend dont know
this guy but Cal lucking 4 him 2 arstim hoo sholtim the gun, and if
it turns owt 2 be Daz Subby-lover Barraclough, Cal gonna killim.

Mick grabs my arm, shoves his face near mine and sez i hoap it's
you Barraclough you roten sod. That Pete woz a frend ov mine see.    10
I'd kill you myself only Cal do it slower. then he larfs again and
wolks of.

Mick you havent maid my day. i got lornorders plus Dred after
me. All i need now is creechers from ota space and fings'll be pretty
tuff.                                                                 15

---

14 **creecher** = creature: a real or imaginary living thing    **ota** = outer

# ZOE

I don't know if you've ever spent any time in a roofspace. If you have
you'll know it can get unbelievably cold at night. I had three thick
blankets, but I used one folded as a mattress and the other two
weren't enough to keep me from shivering most of that first night.
5  Maybe it was fear as much as cold that caused it. I can't tell you what
it's like to be hunted – you'd have to experience it but I hope you
never do. Anyway I didn't get much sleep.

Daytime was worse, in a way. I woke from a doze and somebody
was moving about below. I looked at my watch. It was only eight
10  fifteen so it must be James. My legs and feet were frozen. I sat up and
massaged them and it worked to some extent and then I felt hungry.
I'd drunk more than half the soup last night and when I reopened
the flask the rest was barely warm. I glugged it down, trying not to
think about Mum's pancakes.

15  After breakfast it was plastic bucket by torchlight time. Don't ever
try it.

The kids started arriving at eight forty-five. I don't know how
many there were but they made a terrific racket. I could've boogied
up and down the roof-space playing electric bass and nobody'd have
20  known I was there, but at nine on the dot it all went quiet and for
the next three hours I sat like a stuffed owl, listening for sirens.

At twelve the kids erupted as school recessed for lunch. I expected
a noisy hour in which I'd be able to move about a bit and stretch my
legs, but after a minute or two the whoops and hollers receded and
25  soon the place was silent.

Then there came a knock on the trap which damn near brought
on a heart attack till James's voice said, 'Okay, Zoe – it's only me.'

---

8 **doze**: short period of sleep   13 **glug sth.** (infml): drink sth. quickly   18 **racket**:
loud unpleasant noise   18 **racket** (infml): loud unpleasant noise   **boogie** (v):
dance to fast pop music   21 **stuffed owl**: *ausgestopfte Eule*   22 **erupt**: break
out   **recess** (AE, v) [rɪ'ses]: take a break   24 **whoop** (n): loud cry expressing
joy   **holler** (n): loud shout

He'd brought me lunch – a packet of egg mayonnaise sandwiches which I demolished while he watched from his perch on the rim of the trap. I took a long drink from the can of coke he gave me, then said, 'Where did the kids go?'

He shrugged. 'Home, I guess. They're through for the day.'   5

'School's just mornings?'

'For them it is. Second shift starts one thirty.'

'You mean different kids?'

'Ah-ha. Older. There're not many schools out here, y'know – not nearly enough for all the kids who'd like to come. They all operate   10 the two-shift system but the waiting lists get no shorter.' He smiled. 'I better go. Some eager pupil might arrive early and catch me.'

He took my litter and flask and went, saying he'd look in again after school. I promised myself that if I was still here tonight I'd climb down, empty my bucket and treat myself to a really good   15 wash.

The thought kept me cheerful through afternoon school.

* * *

The second night was better. Instead of soup, James had filled the flask with coffee and there were sandwiches. There was also a hint that I might be out tomorrow, but when I tried to question him he   20 refused to be drawn.

When darkness came I kept the promise I'd made to myself. It was harder than I'd expected because I daren't use the torch and when I opened the trap the step ladder wasn't there. Well, of course it isn't, you idiot, I told myself. He didn't know you were planning to   25 come down, and it'd be a dead givaway if the cops decided to search the school, wouldn't it? He might as well pin up a little card with an arrow on it saying this way to the fugitive.

---

2 **demolish sth.** (BE infml): eat sth. very quickly   **perch**: high seat or position
21 **draw sb.**: make sb. say more about sth.   28 **arrow**: *Pfeil*   **fugitive**: a person who has escaped from somewhere and is trying not to be caught

So what I had to do was lower myself through the trap, hang by my hands and drop. I know what you're thinking. You're thinking, how'd she do that while carrying a plastic bucket, right? Well, I didn't. I dropped empty-handed, dragged out the ladder, set it up
5 and went back for the bucket. Easy, but of course there was a snag – I'd have to leave the ladder in place when I climbed back up, so there was no way I could hide what I was doing. The teacher would know I'd been down.

The water was cold and the one bit of soap I found refused to
10 lather, but I really enjoyed that wash. I even washed my hair as best I could. It wasn't till I'd finished and was wet practically all over that I realised there was no towel. I had to dry myself on one of my blankets and if you think blankets make good towels you're wrong. Anyway, I managed, rubbing away till my body glowed from the
15 friction and I felt better than I'd felt in days. I had to put on the same old dirty clothes afterwards, which was a bit of a bummer but couldn't be helped.

I even slept. Not all night, because it was cold again and I was short one blanket, but I must've zonked for some hours because the
20 night seemed to go in a flash, and as things turned out it was as well I got that rest, because it was going to be a busy day.

To say the least.

---

10 **lather** (of soap): produce small bubbles    15 **friction**: *Reibung*    16 **bummer** (infml): unpleasant situation    19 **zonk** (v, infml): sleep

# DAZ

48    I'm downtown nex day scoring tucker wen I seen this guy i rekernise.
He sees me 2 and coms over. Hear he sez, wots rong wiv that gun
you solt me?

Noffing i sez, why?

2 guys grab me lars nite in the club, he sez. Arst hoo solt it me.    5

Wos 1 of em a littel guy wiv spex?

yea thats rite, and the ovver wos a big 1 wiv mussels.

Did you tel em?

Coudnt coud i – dont know yor name. Tolt em wot you luck lyke
thogh.    10

Fanks.

Yea, well – they luck lyke thay mean biznis, know wot i mean?

I knew wot he ment alrite. i dint hang abowt. Set of hoam fast as
i coud. Lornorders evrywear plus Cal gang lucking 4 me. O Zoe my
lov, if i dont maykit wotl hapen 2 you?    15

Gotta maykit.

1 **score sth.** (v, sl): buy or get sth. illegally

# ZOE

My sleep ended with a bang at eight fifteen as James came storming [49]
up the ladder and flung back the trap. In my fuddled state I thought
it was DS and was trying to crawl into a corner when he barked, 'You
were out last night, weren't you?'

5   'Not out sir,' I said, returning to my blankets. 'I went down for a
wash, and to empty the bucket.'

'You should have asked me. I'd have emptied the damned bucket.
Meant to anyway and forgot. I'd have brought soap and water too, if
you'd mentioned it. I suppose you showed a light?'

10   Boy, was he mad! 'Of course not,' I said. 'I'm not stupid.'

'No? Then why are you here, living like a hunted animal and
putting other people's lives at risk when you could have stayed home
and lived in comfort the rest of your life?'

I looked at him. 'You live in Silverdale too. Why do you come
15   here? You could teach in Silverdale for more money and less hassle,
but you don't.'

'No, I don't.' He sighed. 'Listen, Zoe. I'm sorry I blew up just now,
but I don't think you fully realise what's at stake here. You came out
of Silverdale because you didn't want to move to Peacehaven with
20   your folks. You wanted to stay because you believe yourself to be in
love with Darren Barraclough, and for that you were prepared to put
his life and that of his mother in jeopardy. But there's more at risk
even than that. You've heard of an organization known as FAIR?'

I nodded. 'Yes, and you're a member. Daz told me. And by the
25   way I don't just believe myself in love with him – I am.'

'All right. So you know about FAIR, and you know I'm a member.
Do you know any other members?'

'No.'

'You sure about that?'

30   'Sure I'm sure.' He was starting to sound like Pohlman.

---

18 **be at stake**: *auf dem Spiel stehen*   22 **in jeopardy** ['dʒepədi]: in a dangerous
situation

'What about your friend's father, Wentworth?'

'Oh – oh yeah. I forgot about him.' I hadn't. I just thought it'd be better not to mention him.

'And the lady who wrote this – did you forget her too?' He pulled a crumpled envelope from his pocket and handed it to me. I looked at it. 'There's nothing on this. No writing at all.'

'Open it.'

'Why – what is it?'

'Open it, Zoe.'

I poked my finger under the flap, ripped it across and drew out a flimsy folded sheet which I opened and smoothed out in my lap. It was covered with tiny, cramped writing which looked familiar. I held it up so that light from the trap fell on it and looked at the signature.

Grandma, it said.

\* \* \*

I looked at James. 'You saw my grandmother? She gave you this?'

'Certainly. Your defection has caused problems for us, Zoe. It has stirred up the authorities. Made them nervous. It's difficult for an organization such as ours to operate in such a climate. It's particularly unfortunate that it comes hard on the heels of the Wentworth expulsion which rocked our Silverdale unit to its foundations. It was necessary to discuss your case – to try to find a way of defusing the situation before it gets completely out of hand. That's why your grandmother and I met last night.'

'Are you saying my Grandma's involved with FAIR?'

'Your grandmolher *is* FAIR in Silverdale, Zoe. She founded the unit and ran it virtually single-handed for twenty years, till she decided she was too old and Wentworth took over. Think about it, Zoe – twenty years with a price on her head. Now Wentworth's out

---

5 **crumpled**: *zusammengeknüllt*   10 **flap** (n): *Lasche*   11 **flimsy**: thin
16 **defection**: leaving one country for another that is considered to be an enemy
19 **hard on sth.'s heels**: very soon after sth.   20 **expulsion**: act of forcing sb. to
leave a place   **rock sth. to its foundation**: cause people to question their basic
beliefs about sth.   21 **defuse sth.**: *etwas entschärfen*

and she's back up the sharp end at the age of one hundred and four. Anyway there was this meeting and we think we have a solution. It's not perfect, but it's a lot better than your present predicament.'

'What is it?' I asked the question in a vacant sort of way – my
5   mind was struggling to cope with the idea of Grandma as local head of an illegal organisation. I kept picturing her sweet old face on a wanted poster.

'You're to go to the Wentworth place. You leave tonight. The Barracloughs too, if you can persuade them. If you can't, you must
10  go alone.'

'The Wentworth place? But I don't even know where it is.'

'Your grandmother does.' He nodded at the letter.

'It's all in there.'

'Do the Wentworths know about this?'
15  'Naturally.'

'But how – I mean, Tabby told me the place was miles away. How'd you get in touch?'

'You don't want to know that, Zoe. If you don't make it – if DS get you, then the less you know the better. Read the letter, memorise
20  your grandma's directions and I'll destroy it when I come after school.'

He left some food and went away. I was down. I mean really depressed. In fact I guess you could say I hated myself because he made me see what I'd done. All those people including my own
25  grandmother in danger of their lives because of me. I didn't touch the food – I had no appetite. I sat in the dark, thinking about Grandma and my parents and what it'd be like to see Tabby again. I thought about being caught by DS, too, and wondered what Daz was doing right now. After a while I switched on the torch and read Grandma's
30  letter.

It seemed Wentworth had built his refuge in a place Grandma knew quite well – a much visited beauty spot of sixty, seventy years ago, about thirty miles east of the city. Clanton Rocks, it was called

---

1 **the sharp end of sth.** (infml): the place or position of greatest difficulty or responsibility   3 **predicament** [prɪ'dɪkəment]: difficult situation

in those days. She'd written detailed instructions about how to get there, and there was a sketch map done from memory. She warned that of course things would've changed a lot in the meantime, told me to travel at night if possible and wished me luck. At the end she'd put                                                                                                                      5

'We are members one of another.'

I guess that's a quote but I didn't get it at the time. I cried a bit because these were probably the last words of hers I'd ever have. Then I thought about what a tough little woman she must be to have done all she'd done, and I dried my eyes. Her blood was in my veins,   10 wasn't it? There's a time to cry and a time to be tough, and now it was time to be tough.

When James came again, I'd be ready.

* * *

It was just after three when the cops arrived. I heard a siren but I'd been hearing them for two days, coming closer and closer, then   15 fading as the cars went by.

This one didn't. Its wail swelled till it was like the car was right there in the roof-space, then it cut out abruptly and I heard doors – car doors and school doors, mixed up with voices and footsteps and the sounds excited kids make. Chairs squealed on the plank floor   20 and I pictured cops in the schoolroom, opening, probing, over-turning. Terror held me rigid. Within seconds they'd ransacked the classroom and were directly beneath me. I heard the teacher's voice raised in protest, and another I thought I'd heard before. There was some banging and cursing and milling around, and then somebody   25 said, 'Well – she's gotta be here somewhere,' and it was Pohlman.

I heard them go back to the classroom but I knew they weren't leaving. No way. Not after what Pohlman just said. He'd obviously

---

17 **wail** (n): long loud high cry   21 **probe**: ask questions in order to find out secret or hidden information   22 **rigid**: stiff   **ransack sth.** (for sth.): turn sth. upside down (looking for sth.)

had a tip-off and I knew what he'd do. He'd post somebody outside in case I tried to run, and then he'd lead a far more thorough search. They'd start with the lobby and work their way through the building and nothing – not even the smallest spider – would escape their
5  notice. And when they got to the washroom again Pohlman would see the trap, and smile.

I had to do something. I couldn't just sit shivering like a trapped animal, waiting till they came for me. Because it wasn't just me, was it? It was Grandma and Daz and Mr James and all the others. I might
10  not die if they caught me but others would. Who knows how many in the end? I must take control of my fear and get myself out of this.

In total darkness I crawled, feeling my way to the trap. I hooked my fingers under its rim and raised it ever so slightly. The washroom door was open. I listened. In the schoolroom, kids were talking in
15  subdued tones. Adult voices farther off told me I'd been right – they were searching the lobby, and it wouldn't take long. Then they'd start on the classroom, but would they search it while it was full of kids? I didn't think so, and this gave me an idea. It wasn't a brilliant idea. In fact it was probably a stupid idea which would only get me
20  caught a few minutes sooner than if I stayed where I was, but it was the only thing I could think of so it would have to do.

I eased the trap down gently. Then, risking torchlight for the sake of speed I scooped up blankets, flask and bucket and, bent double, scurried into a far corner where I stood the bucket upside down
25  with the flask inside. The blankets I carried to another corner, pushing them down between joists. Like all roof spaces, this one had its share of accumulated bits and pieces and I hoped the cops wouldn't notice the stuff I'd used. This done, I returned to the trap, doused the light and stuck the torch in the band of my jeans.
30  I raised the trap a little. The washroom was unoccupied. In the classroom a man was yelling at the kids. 'Come on, c'm on – outside. Let's go now.' It was what I'd expected. I raised the trap halfway and eased myself through, supporting the door with my shoulders, the

---

2 **thorough**: very careful   15 **subdued**: quiet   22 **ease sth.**: move sth. slowly and carefully   26 **joist**: *Deckenbalken*   29 **douse a fire** [daʊs]: put out a fire

back of my head and finally on my knuckles. I couldn't prevent the slight bang as it fell into position when I dropped, but the sound was masked by the racket the kids were making as they clattered through scattered chairs and milled around the door.

I breathed a prayer and walked out into the classroom. At the far    5
end a cop stood, fists on hips, watching the push and shove. He wasn't looking my way and I was able to attach myself to the rear of the boisterous scrum. The kids were too busy giving the cops a hard time to notice the new pupil, and I kept my head down as we pushed toward the door.    10

Pohlman was my problem now. In my present filthy state I can't have looked much different from the kids around me, but the lieutenant and I had met. If we came face to face in the lobby it would all be over. I realised that if I was last out or nearly last, I'd be conspicuous. I needed to pass through the lobby in the middle of a    15
surge of kids. I began shoving with my shoulder, worming my way through impossible gaps as I fought my way forward. I got a couple of elbows in the ribs but nobody moaned. Anything that made the cops' job harder was part of the fun.

It wasn't long until the big moment arrived. Jammed momentarily    20
in the creaking doorframe, we exploded into the lobby and were propelled forward on to the backs of those who battled to pass the outer door. I had a glimpse of Pohlman, white with anger, pressed against the wall. He'd probably stationed himself there with the idea of scanning the kids' faces as they passed, but it hadn't worked out    25
that way.

Around the outer door the procedure was repeated. Slowly forward, shoving and being shoved; a brief, asphyxiating hesitation during which I saw, between the heads of those in front, James looking strained with his pupil register tucked under his arm, then    30
explosive release into air and space.

---

1 **knuckle**: *Fingerknöchel*    4 **mill around**: move around without seeming to be going anywhere    8 **boisterous**: noisy and full of life and energy    **scrum**: crowd of people pushing each other    16 **worm your way** [wɜːm]: use a twisting movement to move through a crowded place    22 **battle** (v): fight    28 **asphyxiate sb.** [æs'fɪksɪeɪt]: *jdn. ersticken*

The instant I cleared the doorway I doubled back through hurtling bodies and ran, bent over like in the roof space only faster, to the corner and away along the side of the building. Every moment I expected to hear the command 'halt', but I made it to the next
5   corner and swung round it unchallenged. I was now outside the washroom, with the building between me and everybody else and nothing but derelict land behind. I glanced around. There was nobody in sight, and as long as I stayed close to the wall I couldn't be seen from the washroom window.

10   I breathed in deeply, praying that Pohlman wouldn't decide to walk round the outside of the school. At the far end I heard James calling the roll, kids' voices going sir, sir, sir. I knew the instant Pohlman spotted the trap because he cried out and I heard the drag of the step ladder across the floor, the slam of the trap. As I listened,
15  hardly daring to believe I'd given them the slip, my eyes scanned the terrain. About fifty yards away I saw a small heap of broken bricks. If the worst came to the worst – if they came round this way – that's where I'd go.

   I didn't have to. They slammed around inside for a while, snarling
20  and kicking things, then gave up. Pohlman came out and yelled at James, who wouldn't be too worried about that, but would be wondering how in blue blazes he'd got away with it and what the heck had become of me. When Pohlman was through shouting they got in the car and drove off, and after giving them a minute to get
25  clear I walked away, eating Grandma's letter as I went.

---

1 **double back**: turn back and go in the direction you have come from   2 **hurtle**: move very fast in a particular direction   12 **call the roll**: read a list of names to check who is there   15 **give sb. the slip** (infml): escape from sb. who is following you

# DAZ

50  Cal got our pad staked owt. I seenem frou the windo soonas I got
hoam. 2 guys. 1 on the corner smoaking 1 ded opozit doing noffing.
Mustav seen me com hoam, told Cal. Anityme now Cal orders com
and I know wot. Go in and killim thats wot.

Gotta hyde. Me and Mam. I know wear. Mam I sez. Dred coming   5
4 me I gotta hyde. You 2 I sez cos I know that Cal. He cant find me,
top you insted no hezzy tayshon. Mam scairt. Tekka pill Mam I sez.
She tekka pill, I luck owt the windo seen the 2 guys coming, pockets
fat wiv guns. Com an Mam i sez. no she sez. shex her hed. i vad
enuff our Daz. cant take no more. leev me hear she sez. i got my   10
pills. you go son an god bless.

i dont wanta leaver but no tyme 2 arg you. i hit them baysmen
steps as Cal guys bang frou the doar. they gon up the partmen firs or
i never maykit but I got under that furniss. I dint forgoten Zoe but
cant get up the school no way til Cal guys gon.   15

In the dark waiting I fink ov Zoe in the dark waiting and Mams
god bless and i cry a littel bit. evry 1 cry somtyme even you.

---

1 **pad**: place   7 **hezzy tayshon** = hesitation: *Zögern*   9–10 **i vad enuff** = I've had
enough

# ZOE

Three thirty-five. What I thought I'd do was find a derelict building to hide in till it got dark, then head for Daz's place. Thanks to me, the city was getting a bit too hot for Daz, and I was pretty confident he'd want to go with me to the Wentworth place. I wasn't sure about
5  his mother, though, and I wondered whether he'd leave her if she refused to budge.

I could see a line of gutted houses about half a mile away, and I was heading toward them when I saw a sheet of paper on the ground in front of me. I noticed it because it looked clean and new and
10  because it had my face on it.

I picked it up. It was a sort of handbill. Across the top in big black print was the word **KIDNAP**. Under the picture it said **HAVE YOU SEEN THIS GIRL?** and went on to mention a substantial reward. All you had to do was find a police officer and give your information.
15  I screwed it up and shoved it in my pocket, but when I glanced around to see if anyone had noticed I saw the whole area littered with them. The cops must've flown over in fans, chucking the things out by the handful. It was just what I needed, my picture all over the city.
20  I started to walk faster, keeping my head down. I couldn't actually see anybody but the bills had thrown a scare into me and I was glad when I reached the first of the old houses.

I piled four bricks in a corner and sat on them. I saw a cat and a bird or two but no people. Toward dusk it began to drizzle. The
25  house had no roof. My anorak was supposed to be showerproof but my shoulders were soon wet and so were my knees. By the time it was properly dark I was shivering. I got up and walked toward the city. My jeans clung to my legs and my anorak pockets were wet inside. I comforted myself with the thought that I must look just like
30  a Chippy. I certainly felt like one.

---

3 **hot**: dangerous    6 **budge**: move    7 **gutted**: destroyed inside    13 **substantial**: large    **reward**: amount of money that is offered to sb. for helping the police

It was still raining and there were few people to be seen as I approached the dilapidated block Daz called home. Nevertheless, I didn't go straight up to the door, but stood for a minute or two in the doorway of an abandoned shop, watching and listening. All seemed quiet. No children were playing in the lobby. I shifted my gaze to the damp-scarred face of the building till it found the right window. No light showed there, but this was not unusual. The electricity supply was sporadic because fuel to run the generator was hard to come by, and unreliable because the generator itself was ancient. An hour's uninterrupted current was an event, a full evening of TV virtually unknown. Candles burned in some of the windows but candles, too, were in short supply.

I crossed the road and walked into the dark lobby. It was deserted. The dead elevator wore a shroud of shadow. The stench was familiar now. I took the stairs.

The door of the apartment stood open. I took one step into the hallway and stopped.

'Daz?' No answer.

'Mrs Barraclough?' Silence. The place had an empty feel to it, yet I couldn't believe neither occupant was in. Daz often went out after dark, I knew that, but his mother didn't. Ever. She told me. So she had to be here, unless –.

I heard a small sound behind me but before I could react an arm was thrown round my waist, a hand clamped my mouth and a soft voice murmured in my ear. 'No noise, now. No noise at all, or the world's total of Subbies will fall by one.'

He wasn't a big guy. No taller than me, in fact, but his grip was good. I struggled for a while and lashed out backwards with my foot, but it was no use. He turned me, pushed me back to the stairs and we hobbled down, awkwardly, his mouth in my hair saying, 'Down we go. There's a good girl, now. All the way down.'

He shoved and wrestled me down to the basement where I saw two men, one with a torch and one with a gun. They were near the

---

9 **unreliable**: that cannot be trusted   10 **uninterrupted**: not stopped   **current**: electricity   14 **shroud of sth.** (fml): thing that covers sth.   **stench**: unpleasant smell   28 **lash out**: suddenly try to hit sb.

old furnace. The little guy pushed me toward them. The one with the torch shone it in my eyes.

'Who's this, Cal?'

Cal! So I'm at Cal's mercy now. The merciless Cal.

5 'This?' Cal chuckled. 'Why, this is nothing less than the answer to all our recent prayers, Mick my boy.' He faced the furnace and called, 'Hey, Mister Barraclough. Here's a friend wants to see you.' He removed his hand from over my mouth, grabbed my ear and gave it a twist that damn near tore it off. I screamed.

10 'Zoe?' As Daz called out I saw it all. Dred had come for him and he'd taken refuge where he'd always taken it — in the crawl space under the furnace. They'd found him somehow, but short of dismantling the base brick by brick, there was no way they could've got him out of there. No way, that is, till I came along.

15 Cal released me and I considered making a run for it. If I got away, maybe Daz could hold out till morning when the police would resume their search for me and Cal would he forced to leave. He must've read my mind or something, because he smiled coldly and murmured, 'Don't even think about it. Smithy here's a crack shot.

20 You'd be dead before you hit the floor.' He turned.

'Darren, you're keeping the lady waiting. Where's your manners, lad?'

'If I come out,' said Daz, 'Will you let her go?'

'You have my word, and you know I'm a man of my word.'

25 'What'll you do to him?' I asked, though I guess I knew the answer.

He looked at me. 'Do to him? Why I'm going to kill him of course. What else?'

'Daz,' I cried, 'Don't come out. They'll kill you if you do.'

30 'And we'll kill her if you don't,' countered Cal. 'And we'll get you anyway, in the end.'

---

4 **mercy**: kind or forgiving attitude towards sb.   13 **dismantle**: take apart a machine or structure   19 **a crack shot**: accurate and skilled at shooting

I'm no heroine. D'you know what a heroine would've done right then? A heroine in a book? She'd have made a dash for it, forced 'em to kill her so they had nothing to bargain with. It occurred to me, but I didn't do it. Couldn't. Maybe I don't love Daz enough. I don't know. Anyway, I hope you're never faced with a choice like that. You think about it afterwards and it's heavy. It screws you up.

Daz was coming out. I could hear him scraping the wall, shuffling sideways in the narrow space. Coming out to die. The guy with the torch, Mick, shone it in his face as he emerged. Daz lifted a hand to shield his eyes, looking for Cal.

'Okay, you got me. Let her go.'

Cal smiled. 'All in good time, lad. We don't want her fetching the law before we're through here, now do we?'

Daz squinted at him. 'How long does it take to kill a guy? You'll be through before she's up the stairs.'

Mick sniggered and Cal said, 'Oh no, lad. You don't understand. What we have here is a breakdown of understanding. Killing can be pretty quick, that's true, but it can also be – how shall I put it – dragged out.' He gazed into Daz's eyes. 'Take Pete now. You remember Pete of course – my good friend Pete, whom you shot in the back? Yes, of course you do. Now Pete's death was one of the quick ones. In fact you could say he never knew what hit him. You on the other hand, will know exactly what hits you. We'll begin, I think, with a kneecap. Young Zoe here can watch.' He turned to me, 'Tell me, have you ever seen a kneecap blown off? Have you heard the noise the victim makes? No?' He shook his head, sadly. 'Terrible, it is. I don't even like to think about it.' As he spoke, he drew a revolver from the pocket of his raincoat. He gestured to the two men. 'Bring him over here and keep a good hold of him.' He leered at Daz. 'This is going to hurt you a lot more than it'll hurt me.' He stooped, thrusting the

5

10

15

20

25

30

---

1 **heroine** ['herəʊɪn]: female hero    2 **make a dash for sth.**: go somewhere suddenly and/or quickly    3 **bargain** (v) ['baːgən]: *verhandeln*    12–13 **fetch the law**: call the police    24 **kneecap** (n): *Kniescheibe*    29 **leer at sb.**: look or smile at sb. in an unpleasant way

gun into the crook of Daz's knee. I cringed and turned my face away as the shot rang out.

* * *

The shot, and the agonised scream which followed it echoed deafeningly through the basement. Sick with horror, yet driven by a
5  compulsion I was powerless to resist I turned. Daz, supported by Mick and Smithy, was still on his feet. Cal was kneeling on the floor with his arms wrapped round his stomach, screaming. His broken glasses lay in a crimson splotch on the floor. As I gaped, the two men let go of Daz and turned toward the stairs. I turned, too. Pohlman
10  was crouching on the bottom step with a smoking gun in his fist. Smithy was raising his own weapon when Pohlman fired again. The gunman spun round and crumpled, his pistol skittering away across the cement. Mick, seeing Pohlman momentarily distracted, doused his torch and made a dash for it, knocking the policeman sideways
15  and leaping on to the stairs. There was a shot, a cry and a metallic clatter. A light which had been shining from somewhere behind Pohlman went out and the basement was plunged into blackness.

A grip clamped my arm, Daz yelled, 'Come on!' and I was dragged, totally blind, across the floor. I don't know how he knew
20  where to go, but almost at once I tripped on the first step and then we were climbing. There was a heck of a racket – shouting, shooting, some sort of motor. Anyway, there we were, going up into blackness and then I saw light – a glimmer and some flashes and we were up in the lobby and somebody had a spotlight on it so I couldn't see
25  much more than in the dark.

I'm not sure, but I think we were shot at as we burst out on the street. Who shot at us I don't know – it might've been Dred, or the

---

1 **crook**: *Beuge*   2 **cringe**: move back and/or away from sb./sth. because you are afraid   5 **compulsion**: strong desire to do sth.   8 **crimson**: dark red   **splotch**: large mark or spot   **gape**: stare with your mouth open   12 **skitter**: move very quickly

cops, or both. Or they might've been shooting at each other and we got in the way. Anyway, Dred was there in strength to engage the cops in a fire-fight, and that's what saved us. We ran through the flash and rattle of small arms fire and everybody was too busy keeping their heads down to worry about us. DS had a fan on the roof of the block and as we set off along the street it came swooping down, chasing us with its spotlamp, but when it slowed to keep pace with us it became a soft target for Dred, whose concentrated fire forced it to climb away. We ran on, gasping and sobbing, and when we stopped there was darkness all around and the light was far behind.

We rested briefly to catch our breath and to marvel at our escape. I told Daz about the letter and what had happened at school. Daz hugged me and said I was a hero and I said no, he and his mother were the brave ones, and then suddenly we both burst into tears, which never happens to heroes in the movies.

We weren't safe yet, of course, and so once we'd got our breath back and dried our eyes and decided which way was west we moved on quickly, intent on putting as much distance as possible between ourselves and the city by dawn.

I was hungry, which isn't surprising when you remember I hadn't eaten anything all day unless you're going to count Grandma's letter, but I was too happy to care. We'd almost died, but here we were alive. Instead of the end we were moving toward the beginning of something. I knew we were. I felt it getting closer.

I could feel it getting closer.

---

2 **in strength**: in large numbers ⁀ 12 **marvel at sth.**: be very surprised or impressed by sth.

# DAZ 4 ZOE

There's this hill, right? Pinkney Hill, a few miles west of the city. It's a    52
long climb, but quicker than going round, and beside there're woods
on the far slope where we knew we'd be safe through the day. It was
still dark when we started up, but dawn was breaking as we reached
5   the top.

Well, we stood for a minute looking back, and though the sky
was lightening in that direction the plain was still in shadow. There
was Rawhampton and there was Silverdale, and as we watched, the
bouncers switched off the spot lamps and then it was impossible to
10   tell where the city ended and the suburb began.

# ADDITIONAL TEXT

## *Segregation*

'Ready for school tomorrow, Callum?' Dad said warmly, seemingly oblivious to the instant tension rising up around the table like razor wire.

'Ready as I'll ever be, Dad,' I muttered, pouring myself a glass of milk from the dinner jug so that I wouldn't have to look at anyone.    5

'It'll be tough, son, but at least it's a start. My son is going to Heathcroft High School. Imagine that!' Dad took a deep breath, his chest actually puffing up with pride as he smiled at me.

'I still think he's making a big mistake …' Mum sniffed.

'Well, I don't.' Dad's smile vanished as he turned to Mum.    10

'He doesn't need to go to their schools. We noughts should have our own schools with the same opportunities that the Crosses enjoy,' Mum retorted. 'We don't need to mix with them.'

'What's wrong with mixing?' I asked, surprised.

'It doesn't work,' Mum replied at once. 'As long as the schools are    15 run by Crosses, we'll always be treated as second-class, second-best nothings. We should look after and educate our own, not wait for the Crosses to do it for us.'

'You never used to believe that,' said Dad.

'I'm not as naïve as I used to be – if that's what you mean,' Mum    20 replied.

---

**segregation**: act or policy of separating people of different races, religions or sexes and treating them in a different way    2 **oblivious to sth.**: not aware of sth.
**tension**: feeling of stress that makes it impossible to relax    2–3 **razor wire**: strong wire with sharp blades sticking out *(Nato-Draht)*    4 **mutter**: speak or say sth. in a quiet voice esp. because you are annoyed about sth.    8 **chest puffed up with pride**: *mit stolzgeschwellter Brust*    11 **nought** [nɔːt]: the figure zero; here: person belonging to a group of society    12 **Cross** (here): person belonging to a group of society    13 **retort**: reply quickly, e.g. in an angry way

I opened my mouth to speak but the words wouldn't come. They were just a jumble in my head. If a Cross had said that to me, I'd be accusing them of all sorts. It seemed to me we'd practised segregation for centuries now and that hadn't worked either. What would satisfy
5   all the noughts and the Crosses who felt the same as Mum? Separate countries? Separate planets? How far away was far enough? What was it about the differences in others that scared some people so much?

'Meggie, if our boy is going to get anywhere in this life, he has to
10   go to their schools and learn to play the game by their rules. He just has to be better at it, that's all.'

'That's all?'

'Don't you want something more for your son than we ever had?' Dad asked, annoyed.

15   'How can you ask me that? If you think …'

'I'm sure everything will be fine, Mum. Don't worry,' I interrupted.

Mum clamped her lips together, her expression thunderous. She stood up and went over to the fridge. I could tell from the way she took out the water bottle and slammed the fridge door shut that she
20   wasn't happy. My going to school was the only thing I'd ever heard my parents argue about. Mum twisted the top off the bottle and tipped it so that it was directly over the yellow painted pottery jug she'd made a few weeks back. Water gushed out, rising up in the jug to slosh over the sides and down onto the work surface, but she
25   didn't alter the angle of the bottle.

'You'll soon think you're too good for us.' Jude punched me on the arm for good measure. 'Just don't go getting too big for your boots!'

---

2 **jumble**: untidy or confused mixture of things   3 **accuse sb. of sth.**: say that sb. has done sth. wrong or is guilty of sth.   4 **century**: a hundred years
17 **clamp sth.**: hold sth. very tightly so that it does not move   **thunderous**: looking very angry   25 **alter**: change   **angle**: *Winkel*   26 **punch sb.**: hit sb./sth. with your fist   27 **for good measure**: *obendrein*   27–28 **get too big for your boots**: become too proud of yourself

'Of course he won't. And you'll be on your best behaviour at Heathcroft, won't you?' Dad beamed. 'You'll be representing all of us noughts at the school.'

Why did I have to represent all noughts? Why couldn't I just represent myself?                                                                   5

'You must show them they're wrong about us. Show them we're just as good as they are,' Dad continued.

'He doesn't need to go to their stuck-up school to show them that.' Mum came back to the table, slamming the water jug down on the plastic table cloth.                                                              10

From: Malorie Blackman, *Noughts & Crosses*, London: Corgi Books, 2002, pp. 35–37

---

8 **stuck-up** (adj, infml): thinking that you are more important than other people and behaving in an unfriendly way towards them

# LIST OF WORDS AND PHRASES USED BY DAZ

th [θ] = f (e. g. 'fink' instead of 'think')
th [ð] = v or vv ('bovver' instead of 'bother')

**2** = to/too/two
**4** = for/four
**after (do sth.)** = have to (do sth.)
**a nero** = a hero
**anifing** = anything
**ast** = asked
**aster** = has to
**barf** = bath
**basted** = bastard (n, sl): used to insult sb. *(jdn. beschimpfen)* who has been cruel
**biznis** = business
**bog** (sl): toilet
**bovver** = bother
**Chippy**: person living in the ghetto-like inner cities
**darft** = daft: stupid in a silly way
**dont mean noffing** = doesn't mean nothing = doesn't mean anything
**doodies** (sl, pl): clothes
**Dred**: Chippy rebel organization ready to kill Subbies
**dunnit** = don't it
**encha** = ain't you = aren't you
**fan**: Chippy term for helicopter
**fink** = think
**for Pete's sake** = for God's sake
**goast** = ghost
**graft** (v/n, infml): work
**i aint got** = I haven't got
**innit** = isn't it
**i seen** = I saw *or* I have seen
**it aint** = it isn't
**kilt** = killed

**lornorders** = law and orders: police
**luck** (v) = look
**mebbe** = maybe
**neever** = neither
**not give a monkey's about sb./sth.** (BE sl): not care about sb./sth.
**on your tod** = on your own
**owt** = out
**peanuts**: money
**pertend** = pretend
**seeit** = see-it: identification papers, ID
**speshly** = especially
**Subby**: person living in the suburbs of a city
**thay aint** = they aren't
**thay got** = they have got
**tho** = though
**top sb.** (infml): kill sb.
**tord** = toward
**tork** = talk
**tucker** (infml): food
**tuff** = tough
**veeza** = visa: stamp in your passport giving you permission to enter e.g. a country
**Veeza-Teeza** = visa-teaser: exam that teases Chippies with the possibility of going to a Subby school
**veezavill** = Visaville: Chippy term for a suburb (which you need a visa to enter)
**wot** = what

# THE AUTHOR

Robert Swindells was born in Bradford in West Yorkshire in 1939, the year in which World War II began. As a child he was an avid reader and the only subject he liked at school was English. He left school at the age of 15, joined the Royal Air Force for three years (of which he served two in Germany) and did various odd jobs until 1969. After successfully completing night school, he went to college to become a primary school teacher. He taught until 1980 when he finally dedicated himself to writing full-time.

He has written more than 20 novels for children and young adults, many of which have won literary awards. His novels are often set in a dystopian society and his protagonists are mainly young adults fighting against injustice or poverty. His latest novel, *A Skull in Shadows Lane*, was published in 2012.

Robert Swindells is an activist in the anti-nuclear movement and in 2010 was a candidate for the Green Party in Bradford. He lives in Keighley in West Yorkshire with his wife Brenda.